955 RICHMOND ROAD

An American Memoir

By

Michael P. Moynihan, Jr.

ISBN-10: 0-692-70382-9
ISBN-13: 978-0-692-70382-3

ACKNOWLEDGEMENTS

As always, the unwavering support of my loving wife, Adele, was essential for the achievement of this, my latest endeavor. I would also like to thank several of my friends for their valued assistance in the process of seeing *995 Richmond Road* through to publication. Doris Honochick provided consistent encouragement, availing herself for assistance with organization and development every step of the way. While allowing my voice to remain amidst changes, Emily Gormley assisted with the editorial process. Sharing her creative talent, Lesa Ross developed the cover design.

PREFACE

The knowledge and wisdom that come with age allow the mind's eye to see decades of old memories in a different light. Clarity and forgiveness are to be found in hindsight.

Each of us has our own perspective on what it means to be part of a family. There is no road map or guide book for the structure, interaction, and support we bring one another. We simply rely on what we know: our instincts for love and protection.

Having raised my own family I found myself reflecting on my childhood. To all appearances we were a typical working-class family. Our collective turmoil, however, belied any sense of normalcy.

While reviving the memories of my youth I was flooded with emotions – saddened, puzzled, and angry; while also happy and grateful for having had the good fortune to be a part of this family. I realize now that, troubled as my life may have been, many families were not so different from my own. I was ultimately uplifted by the changing tides of my life. Mine was, in fact, a story of survival.

INTRODUCTION

Rising from a painful era in our country's history sprang the best hope for the future: those who were to become the mid-20th century's social revolutionaries. Hopeful, while bewildered by their progeny's changing values, the venerated greatest generation of World War II watched as their long-held traditions were thrown to the wind.

My family, the Moynihan's, were part of the aspiring masses striving to achieve the (sometimes elusive) American Dream during this pivotal point of political and social change in our country's history. My father, Mike Moynihan, stood at the helm of our family ship. An unpredictable, wild, red-headed Irishman, he was a veteran of the war in the Pacific who steered us through life's storms to the best of his ability, all the while living a life of quiet desperation. Publicly, he fought a lifelong battle with alcohol, anger, and the effects of war. Privately, he struggled with an unspoken need to find a deeper meaning to life beneath the chaos that occupied most of his waking hours.

The course upon which my father steered us made for a choppy ride, a ride filled with waves of emotion. I write about the pains, joys, dreams, and fears we all encountered as we navigated this unpredictable world, as a family. We may not be able to choose our family, but we can – and did – choose to love one another and to make the best of whatever fate brought our way.

955 RICHMOND ROAD

I am but a mortal apprentice in this life, tasked with learning my role in Creation and spreading what peace I can within my world.

– Mickey Moynihan

East Stroudsburg, Pennsylvania
Thanksgiving 2014

In preparation for Thanksgiving dinner, my wife, Adele, and I readied our well-preserved antique oak table for soon-to-arrive family and friends. The table, a resident and a rallying point in Moynihan homes for the past half-century, now served me here in Pennsylvania, a long way from and many years after our initial meeting. As we set places on the old oaken surface that had weathered many a year's meals, meetings, and holiday celebrations, nostalgia caught hold of me. I was moved by the impressive history associated with this centerpiece of our dining room.

As Adele continued preparations for our company, I paused to sit in one of the six sturdy captain's chairs that stand guard around our beloved table. Viewing the remaining five empty chairs – vigilant at their assigned posts – I began to reminisce about my life and about the people who had occupied those chairs over the years. My father, long since gone, seemed to dominate my vision as I focused on the broad landscape of events and faces that found their way to this table's side. It was fitting that my father should dominate these memories; after all, it was he who first introduced the revered table into our home. He was the head of our family; a strong, remarkable person who bore the vision of a genius and the behavior of a madman. Together with my mother and my two brothers and sister, we were the Moynihan's.

1

My first glimpse of the venerable table was way back in 1960. My father had unexpectedly pulled up to our new home at 955 Richmond Road on Staten Island with the table perched haphazardly atop his prized Ford Galaxy. Clothes' line crisscrossed the car's roof like a spider web, holding the inverted table, its large eagle-claw legs reaching for the sky, with only the slightest of assurances. Bulging from within the car's interior and reaching out from the trunk were the accompanying chairs. Its arrival was undignified given its hardwood stature; but, despite the awkward introduction, I could see that the table was a fine piece of work. My father proudly proclaimed its arrival: "How do you like that?!"

Not expecting something like this to be accompanying him to our door, we listened intently as my father proceeded to tell the story of how he acquired the treasure. He had, in fact, discovered it abandoned at the curb of a Victorian mansion in a neighborhood once home to wealthy merchants. The former owners, who controlled a major shipping line, had simply discarded it as trash. A caretaker for the property told my father it was his if he wanted it; and so, with the help of the caretaker, the prized table soon found its way to the roof of its new owner's car. Not wanting it to travel without its loyal companions, they loaded up the chairs as well. After a bumpy journey along cobblestone streets, the table and chairs came to rest at their new home. How fitting it was for them to join us here at this time as we, ourselves, had only recently moved in; we were all strangers of sorts to this place.

I gave my dad a hand untying our new resident. In his haste to get the valuable adopted furniture home, he had tied knots that somehow became permanent lumps in the clothes' line tether. We had to cut the table to freedom; it seemed to give an audible sigh of relief once unshackled. With the help of my older brother, Fred, we carefully removed it from its undignified inverted position and, under the watchful eye of my mother, made our way up the ancient slate walkway that led to our front door. Greeting us there, our dog gave a sniff of approval as we entered the house. Our old table was pushed aside, destined to face the same curbside fate as this one my father had rescued. The new table fit perfectly and seemed at ease beside the old stone fireplace in our large kitchen.

Upon close examination we discovered the table had suffered some injuries in transport. Carefully, like a nurse attending to an injured patient, my mother applied some Old English wood polish with a small cloth to rejuvenate the injured oak. Once healed, our chairs were placed around the table. We all sat to begin bonding with this welcome addition to our new home. We each had an assigned seat at the table. Like a pecking order in the animal kingdom, once designated those seats would remain permanent until we left the flock. After some time my father leaned back in his chair with an air of contentment; it creaked as he brought it to sit on its two back legs. "Please don't do that," my mother exclaimed, "you could damage the legs. And if they break, you will also damage your head."

Already respected amidst our other furnishings, this table was assigned an elevated stature in the furniture hierarchy of our humble home. For years to come, it would serve as our anchor, maintaining its quiet presence while absorbing our pains and radiating our joys. This table would host a last meal for both me and my brother before we went off to war; and, fortunately, it would welcome us when we returned home. We would gather here not only to share meals but to share our enthusiasms and hopes for the future. This table would accompany our family as we began to fulfill our own American Dream.

Only some few months back, we had been living in a city housing project in South Beach, a small town on Staten Island. We had moved there from New York City around 14 years earlier. It was a move necessitated by circumstances that were never fully clear to me. The best I could surmise was that we had seemingly fled to the suburbs for a better and safer life because my father, in his penchant for heavy drinking and fighting, had apparently crossed the wrong sort of people in New York City.

South Beach Projects, Staten Island
Late 1950's

City housing projects like ours had sprung up all across New York City post-World War II; they were an oasis for the growing families of returning serviceman. Populated with a variety of ethnic groups, they were true melting pots of first- and second-generation immigrants. Residents were typically lower- to middle-income blue-collar workers – many of them New York City cops, firemen, and sanitation workers – all expressing a desire to advance and grow in the economic expansion that followed the war. The projects, although viewed by many with a negative stigma, boasted quite a positive sense of community. In many ways those living in your building became your extended family. Going to a neighbor to borrow a cup of sugar or some milk was a common experience, as was babysitting each other's kids or loaning someone a few dollars until payday. Everyone seemed to share similar needs, and there was an underlying sense of unity in this community of close living.

Our modest apartment was small but functional with three bedrooms and one bath. The shortage of room in those project apartments always sent the children of the budding families into the courtyards and playgrounds that surrounded the buildings. Children's voices, laughter, and songs frequently filled the air and echoed amidst the canyons of brick and glass that were our landscape. The courtyards were always occupied with old men playing checkers, kids playing hopscotch on the concrete (on makeshift chalk drawings), and big baby carriages that were often carrying several occupants. These communal spaces allowed for simple, unscripted gatherings, bringing the 36 families of each building into a daily social mix whenever they just wanted to pass the time.

4

The apartments that boasted the luxury of a television were clearly indicated by the large, unsightly antennae – an accepted blight to the eye – that extended from their windows. If you owned a set in those days, like we did, you were considered well-off. The television did little to keep us indoors, as there were but a few stations to watch and the screens were always plagued by periodic static and fluttering lines; but we appreciated the comfort. We were also fortunate to have a telephone. Even though it was a party-line phone (which meant we shared the line with others, prone to interruption and eavesdropping), it sure beat having to go down to the street to use a pay phone.

Summers in the projects were unforgettable. Given the high concentration of kids, we always had an ample supply of players for whatever sport was the focus of the day. At that time the only air-conditioning available was an open window; and so the summer heat would drive everyone out of their buildings to congregate on the green wooden benches scattered throughout the courtyards. Trips to the beach or to the city pool provided an alternate escape from the stifling heat in our apartments. The highlight of every summer evening, of course, was the arrival of the Good Humor ice cream truck. It was an ice-cream parlor on wheels whose distinctive ringing bell made its presence known long before we could see it; the effect of that bell was Pavlovian on both young and old alike. Kids would all tug at their parents, pleading for some change for ice cream. Disappointment would reign on the faces of those who would come up short of money, but their spirits were often uplifted by a friend who would share half of their popular two-stick Popsicle bar. Waiting anxiously as the truck pulled up to the curb, a line of eager customers would be counting their change and scanning the choices and prices posted on the side of the truck. Dressed in all white, topped with his trademark white hat, the ice cream man would exit his coach to attend to his clients. He would move quickly and mechanically, opening the small door that allowed access to the cache of frozen treats within the dry ice cavern; a cool, white cloud would escape each time that door was opened. All the while, the silver change dispenser attached to his belt clicked away, and he would keep yelling out in an authoritative voice for us to figure out what we wanted while we were waiting; inevitably, though, there was always some indecisive youngster who would eventually hold up the line.

Winters in the projects were just as memorable. Whenever it got really cold outside, the inside of our windows (lacking any insulation) would be covered in ice to the point where they looked like a freezer in serious need of defrosting; but no one cared. Winter gave us the opportunity to do battle with adjoining buildings in massive snowball fights and to take part in the construction of huge snow forts.

In the late 1950's and early 1960's a new form of music had arrived on the scene: rock 'n roll. The music industry, and the world for that matter, would never be the same. Street corners were filled with groups of four or five crooners all seeking to become the next big thing on American Bandstand. Beneath our windows, from six floors below, we would often hear aspiring groups practicing their songs. Over and over again the songs would be repeated until they achieved the sought-after harmony. The voice of the falsetto lead singers would pierce the evening air with their strident overtures. The acoustics of the buildings' courtyards created a favorable resonance for such *a cappella* performers (accompanied solely by their snapping fingers or clapping hands). Their serenades would usually coincide with the time we went to bed, offering a distraction – a lullaby of sorts – while we awaited sleep. On occasion you would hear a yell from one of the surrounding buildings calling for the group to "Shut the hell up!" but most people seemed to enjoy the free, unscheduled performances. Some groups actually hit the big time with the songs that had so often echoed throughout the outdoor studio below our apartment. I especially remember The Elegants doing just that with their song "Little Star."

Traveling anywhere outside of our own neighborhood was something that did not occur very often in those days. A few times a year we would travel from Staten Island to New York

City to visit my father's parents; to get there we would take the Staten Island Ferry. The ferry was our main link to the city. It was seen as a "commuter cruise" for those who rode it each day to get to work. The ferry was huge; it could carry 1,000 people and a good number of cars. It could make the trip to Manhattan in 20 minutes and, at that time, cost only five cents. I remember the deckhands carrying out their duties in response to the different bells that would sound alerting them to cast off their moorings. Once untethered, the ferry would shudder; and the startling loud horn would sound to signal our departure from the slip. The strong smell of the salt air churned up by the powerful propellers that sent the ferry on its way was always present. I would welcome that fresh, salty air and draw it close in deep breaths. If it was a good day, we would get a hot pretzel from the small concession stand on board. The cast of characters on the ferry were many, and they reflected every segment of society: men in three-piece suits with very shiny shoes on their way to Wall Street, construction workers in their finest work garb, your average John and Jane Does, and the sporadic unruly drunk or homeless man. Of course there were also the occasional groups of tourists, cameras fluttering all the while as their foreign speech drew looks of interest from us locals.

When the weather permitted, we wanted to be sitting outdoors on the left side of the ferry (starboard, as the deckhands would say) on our voyages to Manhattan. From there we could see the Statue of Liberty as she stood tall and straight, keeping watch over all the activity in the harbor. We were always awestruck while watching downtown Manhattan grow steadily larger as we neared the great city. The massive buildings of steel, glass, and concrete were, in their own way, magical. The ferry ride was always over too soon. It typically ended with the bunching of people at the front of the ferry and, because of the strong currents, an inevitable bang into the huge wooden pilings wrapped with thick rope. I enjoyed our occasional ferry rides into Manhattan. I don't know if the air was cleaner or if the sun shined brighter in those days, but in my memory it seemed as such.

Life in the projects, at that time, was one of quiet, contented struggle. Each family sought to reach a point where they could move on – to be free of noisy neighbors, slow elevators, and no growing equity. You had to own a home – it was the American Dream. Having found sobriety and seeing clearly for the first time since the war in the Pacific, my father came alive in the prospect of owning his own home. Over the years we had watched many of our friends take the plunge into the world of home ownership (some even moving as far away as New Jersey). When someone moved, it was always cause for celebration as we were always hopeful we would be next. Our turn finally came in the spring of 1960.

My parents had found an unusual piece of real estate. Historically speaking, it was quite a find: built in 1756, it was one of the oldest homes on Staten Island. In terms of restoration, it was a nightmare. The front part of the home had suffered from fire and was never repaired. The yard was filled with junk, and knee-high grass covered the landscape. It was a scourge in an otherwise nice neighborhood; yet my parents talked about the house in glowing terms. Blinded by enthusiasm, it was hard for them to see anything but potential in this historic, grand old home. They were excited and prepared to endure whatever work or trials homeownership might entail. When the rest of the family first set eyes on our new castle, however, we were a little unsure how to react. I guess we all had different ways of seeing this opportunity: my brother Fred asked if we could get a dog; I wanted to know if I could have my own room; my sister, Annie, asked how many bathrooms the house had; and my younger brother, Jimmy, well, he was just content to go along with our contagious enthusiasm.

The house came with an impressive list of stories regarding its long history. It was built with the help of local Indians who still inhabited Staten Island during the period of its construction. It housed English troops during the revolution. It served as a toll house and was part of the Underground Railroad. It was once owned by a physicist who corresponded regularly with the famed physicist Albert Einstein. It was also rumored to be haunted. There was a long list of other interesting (and some not so interesting) anecdotes. We embraced these stories as our own and, over time, added an Irish embellishment.

Bolstered by the significance of our new home, we prepared for our relocation from the projects. Spreading the news of our departure was bittersweet. We were excited to be moving but sad to be leaving those with whom we had shared the seasons of our childhood. Fortunately, we would not have to part with our schoolmates as we would continue to attend St. Sylvester's Catholic School, our anchor in education.

We saw St. Sylvester's as a religious military academy. Strict was the order of the day in this no-nonsense system run by the Presentation Order of nuns. They ruled through fear and Catholic guilt, turning out not only educated and morally-sound citizens, but heavily-disciplined and traumatized ones who would long carry the nuns in their memories. In their defense, our class alone had 50 students; and so maintaining control certainly must have required the strong regime.

Our attendance at the school was not always smooth sailing. My brother Fred (who was only a year older than me) was wild. In fact, he held the great distinction of committing one of the top 10 transgressions that would surely put a child on the path to damnation at St. Sylvester's School. It all started one morning as we were tossing a ball around while we waited for the school bus. While retrieving the ball from a nearby area where people dumped their trash, he happened upon a large pile of Playboy magazines. After a wide-eyed look at his discovery, he gathered the valuable cache and carried them back to the bus stop. Circling around him like we would a quarterback in a huddle, he proudly – and with our undivided attention – displayed his find. As the school bus neared, he stuffed them into his school bag, destined to give them further examination and (if you will) exposure at school. He could hardly contain himself. After all, how often does a Catholic schoolboy come upon such prized material? It wasn't long after he took his seat in his seventh grade classroom that the devil got the best of him: he began to discreetly pass the magazines out amongst his favorite classmates. What a travesty! What an abomination! What a terrific way to break the boredom of a history class. Mind you, the classic Catholic nun literally had eyes in the back of her head and rarely missed a beat of what was going on in her classroom; and so it took but a very few minutes for Sister James to realize that the expressions on her students' faces were not the result of a fascinating passage on Lincoln in the history books they held high on their desks. Quicker than anyone could say "uh-oh," she had her hands on the illicit material. The initial pale look of shock on her face quickly turned to a crimson red rage. Fire and brimstone filled her eyes. Sister James was considered the enforcer at our school; she was feared by all. There were tales of her beating people up through the years; some suggested that she passed as a boy before becoming a nun and had fought in the Golden Gloves in New York City. There were even rumors that she probably shaved every morning. Such were our youthful impressions of our cloistered guardians and teachers.

An instant after Sister James asked the class who brought the magazines to school, all eyes fell upon Frederick Joseph Moynihan. He was about to feel her wrath. Her first course of action was to work her way around the clutter of desks – they were my brother's only protection. Sister James was surprisingly quick on her feet; she navigated the narrow aisles between the desks like a ballerina. When she arrived at my brother's desk, she proceeded to beat the crap out of him. Though Fred raised his arms up in defensive mode and managed to deflect many of the blows to his head, quite a few found their mark. Amidst each of her deliberate strikes, Sister James' muffled words of condemnation delivered a truly poor accounting of his character, his sinful disrespect, and his disgraceful behavior. After being thoroughly beaten, and with a startled history class now sitting in silent disbelief, Fred was dragged from his seat and ushered to the dreaded principal's office for perpetrating a Class A religious felony.

Sister Mary De Chantel was our principal. She was an old-school, no-nonsense, smack-you-in-the-face kind of nun. As the

10

story went, she had notches on the belt she wore around her waist to mark the number of kids she knocked out while teaching in a New York City ghetto during the Depression. Holding my brother by his shirt collar, nearly choking him to death, Sister James gave a compulsory quick knock on the principal's door before hurling him into the office. This was the inner sanctum, the holy headquarters of the school, a place you never wanted to be...especially if you were in trouble. I knew this from personal experience.

Some months earlier I had been summoned to the principal's office to face my own interrogation. Although I was uncertain about what was going to happen when I arrived, I knew that I had not done anything for which I should be worried. Unbeknownst to me, however, there was good reason for concern. Sister De Chantel had received a report from an anonymous source that claimed I had consumed a quart of altar wine in my duties as an altar boy. She dropped the charges on me in her typical harsh manner, accusing me and convicting me all in one breath. "Not me, Sister" was all I could say.

"Sit down, Mr. Moynihan." A lone wooden chair in the middle of her office beckoned as the witness stand for my interrogation. I sat, as directed, in nervous anticipation of what was to come. The nun who had escorted me to the office stood off to the side, silently watching as Sister De Chantel began circling the chair and asking me questions. It was so uncomfortable; all the while, she fidgeted with the large rosary beads that hung from her waist, her black vestments brushed against me, and her heels slowly clicked on the tile floor. Suddenly, she diverted from her circumnavigation and confronted me head-on, but a few inches from my face, screaming, "Tell the truth! I know you drank the wine! Admit it!" At 11 years old I wouldn't have been able to consume that much wine if I had wanted to, but Sister De Chantel didn't see it that way. As far as she was concerned, I was the culprit.

"It wasn't me, Sister!"

"Don't lie to me, Mr. Moynihan!"

"I never drank any wine."

After some more prolonged questioning, I could see that the cards were clearly stacked against me. I felt the only way to end the interrogation would be to satisfy the prosecution's case by confessing I was guilty as charged; and so I gave in.

"Okay, I drank the wine."

"I knew it," she said. "You should be ashamed of yourself! I am calling your mother right now to tell her what you have done."

Sister De Chantel then flipped through her Rolodex files to look for my mother's phone number. She dialed a big, black rotary phone that sat off to one side of her orderly, spotless desk. I was more than a little nervous as she firmly and deliberately spun the numbers on the old phone; she seemed to be rising in temperature with each move. It was painful to hear each number clicked off, knowing that each one brought my false conviction that much closer to my mother's ears.

"Hello, Mrs. Moynihan. This is Sister Mary De Chantel, the principal at St. Sylvester's School...I'm fine, thank you. I have some bad news regarding your son Michael. We have discovered that Michael drank a quart of altar wine while in the church before a Mass."

I wasn't sure what Mass she was referring to; but, if I had drunk a quart of wine, I would certainly not have made it to the altar. There was some conversation back and forth; at one point Sister even seemed flummoxed for a moment. "Mrs. Moynihan, this is a very serious matter. I will have to tell Monsignor Dalton. Thank you very much. Goodbye." After she hung up, she said, "Okay, Mr. Moynihan, back to class. I will alert Monsignor about what you have done. You should go to confession as soon as possible. And you will probably no longer be able to serve Mass." That was a consequence that I did not see coming; it came as a shock to me.

I rose from my fateful chair with the resounding threat of being excommunicated from the altar boys echoing in my mind. This was a tragic event for an 11-year-old Irishman in a Catholic school. After all, who gets removed from such a service? It would surely be hard to explain. As it turned out, I would be ostracized by some of my peers, but I would be hailed as a hero amongst the rest.

The Monsignor was a very old and crotchety man. When I met with him, he assured me that nothing like this would ever happen again because I would no longer be allowed to perform the services of an altar boy. As predicted, I got my pink slip...so much for learning all the Latin responses for the Mass, and so much for forgiveness. Not too long after my expulsion from the altar service, the school janitor (who also took care of the church) was found passed-out drunk in a church pew. Several empty bottles of altar wine were found amidst his cleaning equipment. He had clearly consumed the wine as he cleaned the church at night. Alas, the janitor was the guilty party for whom I had taken the fall.

My reputation remained tarnished. I was never reinstated to my former position as an altar boy, nor was I ever given a formal apology. I was, however, exonerated in my own mind, and I carried the experience as a badge of honor. My mother had known all along that I couldn't have drunk the wine. In fact, years later, she told me about her short conversation with Sister De Chantel. Apparently, after Sister had leveled her charges – in that moment when I had noticed she looked flummoxed – my mother had asked lightheartedly whether or not she "would recommend AA." Sister had clearly not been amused. That was my sole experience in the principal's office; fortunately, the unwarranted visit proved to be a short-lived trauma, leaving me none the worse for wear.

My brother Fred's visit, on the other hand, was justifiable. He had earned his trip to Sister De Chantel's office by sharing those illicit magazines with his class. A great storyteller, he recounted the events of his own inquisition in that dreaded room with such vivid detail that I remember feeling like I was right there with him.

It was no ordinary room. There was the faint smell of burning wax and incense wafting through the air. As an altar boy, it was a familiar smell that reminded him of the nearby church where he would serve Mass on Sundays. Every inch of the small office was filled with religious icons that had been gathered over scores of years: statues, crosses, and glorious, golden-framed pictures of Mary and Jesus. There were pictures of the Pope and Cardinal of New York that served to enhance the atmosphere of religious authority. Fred was not a stranger to this office. As Sister James hurled my brother into the room for this latest transgression, he sought to project his best schoolboy countenance of innocence despite the swelling red marks she had left on his face. Sister Mary De Chantel peered out from the traditional garb that designated her religious order. The old, bespectacled, short, and overweight principal looked up from behind her desk and asked, "Yes, Sister James, what is this about?"

Her words charged with indignation, Sister James recounted the incident in class. Placing the contraband as evidence on the principal's desk, she proclaimed, "Here they are, Sister. Filthy books. What a disgrace!"

My brother said he would not have been surprised if the magazines had exploded into flames at that very moment under Sister De Chantel's powerful glance. "You horrible, horrible, sinful, sinful, dirty little boy!" His recollection of her exact words was not all that clear, but he was pretty sure she went on to tell him that he was going to Hell. This was a mortal sin of the gravest nature, and it would be dealt with harshly. It was likely grounds for expulsion. My brother maintained his adolescent composure while being thoroughly grilled by these two seasoned nuns, both equally skilled in extracting information from wayward, young minds.

"Where did you get these magazines? Did you steal them from Kazucchi's?"

Kazucchi's was a trashy local deli frequented by many students from St. Sylvester's. It held the distinction (at least in our minds) of being the dirtiest deli in New York City. Much like the store itself, Mr. Kazucchi was slovenly – overweight, unshaven, and usually with a long-ashed cigarette hanging from his mouth. On one occasion we witnessed Mr. Kazucchi, while making a hero sandwich on his filthy cutting board, calmly severe the head of a huge cockroach with his large cutting knife like a ninja warrior. He casually scraped the aftermath on his soiled apron and proceeded to cut the sandwich. It was truly a disgusting place; but we were kids, and the baloney sandwiches were cheap. The large variety of skin magazines offered at the deli did little to improve its filthy ambience.

Sister James and Sister De Chantel continued to rapidly fire questions at Fred in an attempt to disrupt his thinking process. Each of his forced, quick replies gave them ammunition for further interrogation. The truth was his only defense: "I found them in a trash pile near the South Beach projects."

"Don't lie to us. We know you stole them from Kazucchi's!"

Holding strong, Fred insisted that he had found the magazines while we waited for the bus. Apparently, such a simple scenario did not satiate their need to hear of some more nefarious way in which the Devil must have interacted with this young man; and so the interrogation continued. Fred expected to be flogged or doused with holy water at any moment. Given the highly-charged atmosphere, he also considered the distinct possibility that lightning bolts could burst from the religious artifacts that graced the walls. Together those two nuns worked my brother over until they tired themselves out. When they finally stepped out of the room to regroup, Fred saw his chance to break free of the inquisition and bolted. Such was his fear of what might come next; he sped down the hall, past the statue of St. Sylvester, and straight out the front door into the winter cold, without his coat. He made his way several miles to our home in the projects. His early, and coatless, arrival home prompted my mother to call the school to ask for an explanation. Sister De Chantel was more than willing to oblige. She shared Fred's transgressions with my mother, leaving her with little to say other than that she would be sending him back to school on the city bus and asking that when he left school the next time, someone could "please make sure he has his jacket on." After a mandatory meeting with Monsignor Dalton, a trip to the confessional, a lengthy set of prayers, a humiliating trip by my mother to the school, and some other yet-to-be-determined punishments, it was decided that Fred could remain at St. Sylvester's.

My brother Fred was a tough act to follow. He was impulsive and crazy; the nuns described him as "incorrigible." As we younger Moynihan's moved through the higher grades at St. Sylvester's, we would always be reminded when under the tutelage of a new nun that we were "oh, Frederick Moynihan's" brother or sister. Their recognition was always spoken with an emphasis that assured us our family name carried an asterisk associating us with those infamous Playboy magazines.

Staten Island, New York
Early 1960's

Moving day was upon us at long last. Excitedly – though admittedly with some trepidation – we loaded our belongings onto a truck. Many of the neighbors and friends we had known throughout our childhood were on hand to help. We had been part of a true neighborhood – a network of friendships and memories – here in the projects; but, though we were sorry to say goodbye, we were happy to be moving on to our new home. A piece of the American Dream was now in our grasp.

We were all excited as we pulled up in front of our new house. The old moving truck and our small caravan of helpers and well-wishers lined the curb in front of our new residence at 955 Richmond Road. My parents' optimism was contagious; it spread through the rest of the family. I felt we were bonded in a way we had never been before – much more united as a family – and it was a very good feeling. Despite the burnt-out area of one section of the house and the massive amount of cosmetic work that would obviously need to be done, we all had but one vision of this diamond in the rough: it was ours.

We all hurried up the thick slate walkway that led to our new home's entrance. There before us was an ancient, well-weathered oak door covering a threshold set between large stone walls laid several hundred years earlier. We would cross that threshold as a family. My father had the honor of leading the way. He used a big, old brass key to free the lock with a loud click. Immediately upon entering we could feel a warm presence, as if the house itself were welcoming us. It felt good to be home.

We worked our way through the house and were assigned our rooms. It was determined that Fred and I would share a room on the second floor, with my sister Annie down the hall. My parents would reside on the first floor, as would my younger brother, Jimmy. Our modest furnishings brought a sense of familiarity into our new home, but they seemed lost given the size of the rooms. I could not believe how big all the rooms in this house were. The attic alone was bigger than our old apartment. The basement not only housed a huge coal furnace that could surely heat the entire house, but it also boasted an extra-special feature: another mysterious, secret basement hidden below a trap door! It was very cool. This house was going to be a fascinating place to live: there were long hallways with multiple doors, spacious rooms, high ceilings, steps that creaked, large box windows, and old fireplaces that had warmed huddled families for over two centuries. Come our first nightfall, the house would introduce us to a whole other host of unfamiliar shadows and sounds seemingly reserved for the darkness. This house, with its long history, had sheltered numerous generations over its lifetime – and now it was time to make it our own.

We had settled in by late springtime; now the real work was about to begin. We soon discovered that one of the drawbacks to having lived in an apartment for so many years (with a super responsible for our home repairs) was that my father had never developed the ways of a handyman. Although he was a steelworker, my father lacked the proper tools and expertise required to complete many of the necessary repairs at our new home. That lack of skill led to the inevitable frustrations which resulted in his fairly regular refrain of *"Son of a bitch!"* during the course of many a weekend repair job.

The yard seemed to be the most daunting of projects as there was an abundance of human and organic trash to address. We proceeded to cut everything that was not moving across our half-acre lot with our new lawnmower. Piles and piles of brush and junk lined the curb in front of our house. Considering the size of those waste piles, it all probably should have been hauled off by private carriers; but I think my father gave the city garbage collectors a few extra bucks to encourage them to remove it for us. Progress was slow but steady. After some weeks we had the makings of a fine yard. We even turned the soil to establish our first garden; we felt like true pioneers when that garden eventually produced our first tomato plants.

***

For some reason the smell of fresh coffee always enlivens the senses. It is an aroma that brings about an anticipation of something to come: perhaps a meal, a quick pick me up, or simply the occasion to sit around with friends and pass the time. In our house the smell of coffee marked two very specific things: the start of a new day, when it seemed to find its way throughout the house like a sensory alarm clock; and that time around dinner when someone would inevitably arrive to meet with my father to talk and then go with him to an AA meeting.

The pleasant aroma of coffee wafting through our home was typically accompanied by the less appealing smell of cigarette smoke. Ashtrays always seemed readily available around our kitchen as the majority of those who set their feet beneath our table were smokers. My father's personal choice of poison was the short, unfiltered, hardcore cigarettes called Lucky Strike. Recognized internationally after World War II (as they had been supplied with the troop's C rations) Lucky Strikes were considered the "true man's cigarette," a hallmark of U.S. tobacco quality. As many of those men would learn the hard way, however, these cigarettes were also deadly to longtime smokers.

Nicotine addiction was widespread in the 1960s; it permeated all levels of society. Smoking was not seen as quite so offensive back then as it is today; rather it was an expected experience after a big meal, a cup of coffee, with a beer, or during periodic work breaks (shoot, you could even smoke on an airplane). Smoking was enticing. It was seen as a benign yet loathsome gift from the greatest generation; but it was an addictive and deadly tradition that quietly invited various lethal cancers to take hold of many lives. I often wonder how our society could be so knowledgeable, yet so misguided as to entertain such a self-destructive habit.

I began learning about the impact of addictions at a very young age. At first I knew precious little about the AA program other than it was important for people like my father who had a problem with drinking. My father's involvement in Alcoholics Anonymous, or "the program" as it was referred to by members, began when he admitted that he was powerless over alcohol and had given up the fight to control his drinking. Reaching that point had taken probably 20 years – 20 whole years of self-destructive behavior that had eroded his physical, mental, and spiritual integrity; not to mention the negative impact it had on his family, friends, and anyone who came into contact with him.

The reach of alcoholism is far beyond the alcoholic. Accidents on the highways and in the workplace were (and remain) on the top of the list for fatalities caused by drinking. Crime and the attendant prison population furnish further testament to the impact of the bottle on our society; a great number of felons inspired by the bottle were often so drunk they wouldn't even remember committing their crimes. But, socially, the family of the alcoholic – those with whom they shared a home – bore the brunt of the immediate and long-term damaging effects of alcoholism.

On any given night that we sat – young and impressionable – at our dinner table, we were likely to encounter the lost, lonely, and sick faces of those who were ravaged by alcohol. Over the years we became accustomed with those who suffered; they were often hopeless and desperately seeking relief from this all-consuming addiction. We recognized that each person may have shared the same sickness, but they each suffered differently. We also came to realize there was no part of society that escaped addiction: priests and criminals; proud, angry, and listless; rich and poor; black and white; young and old; smart and uneducated. They all crossed our threshold and found their way to our cherished table, where they were offered a meal, a cup of coffee, and some kindness. Anyone seeking help was welcomed.

The procession of characters around our kitchen table was diverse, unusual, and bizarre. They each served as an illustration of how badly the human body and mind could be damaged through addiction. Though many people not lured by alcohol only see a drunkard's affliction as the result of a lack of willpower or reckless self-indulgence, I understood from a very young age that there was much more to it than that. These people had a predisposition to alcoholism; they were suffering from a disease related to this ages-old fermented beverage. I watched firsthand as this much-loved elixir caressed countless people into lives of endless suffering and early deaths. Through the years alcohol has clearly eaten away at the souls of legions of families, scarring young and old alike. Sadly, I can especially empathize with the young innocent souls, minds, and hearts that have been darkened by the traumas inherent to having an alcoholic parent.

In spite of all his insanity my father had found a niche where he excelled: helping people recover from alcohol. He was very good at his vocation, especially with those who were hardcore cases. Criminals of the worst sort, who others could not or would not reach out to, found a friend in the tough love of Mean Mike (a well-earned title he proudly wore, though no one would refer to him as such face-to-face). My father had a peculiar ability to spot a weakness – a sensitivity – within people that he could exploit as an entry point past their strongest emotional defenses. He could then reach inside an addicted mind and resurrect the human spirit that was living in a darkness where it had ceased to function. My father had a true gift.

Manhattan, New York
Early 1900's

My grandfather's arrival on these shores was supposedly prompted by an incident involving the IRA. Shortly after traveling via steamer to the land of opportunity and obscurity, Humphrey Joseph Moynihan met and fell in love with his future wife, Hannah O'Leary, a fellow recent immigrant from Ireland. In keeping with the tradition of immigrants of that time, he worked hard to provide for his family. He was an industrious entrepreneur who owned several horse-drawn carriages and ran a successful business ferrying people around Central Park. His occasional odd behavior and personality were attributed to a direct kick to the head by a mule in a stable in his native Ireland.

My father, born in 1918, was the second of four children blessed upon Humphrey and Hannah. Along with his two brothers and sister, he was raised on the Upper West Side of Manhattan. The children of strict Irish Catholic immigrants who had arrived in this country in pursuit of the American Dream, they had a fairly comfortable childhood complete with an austere Catholic education and an adequate share of its complementary Catholic guilt.

They grew up amidst a tumultuous period in our country's history. World War II had created a stir of nationalism throughout the American population, and the Moynihan boys were caught up in the ensuing tide of youthful military volunteers after the Japanese attack on Pearl Harbor. All three heeded the call of Uncle Sam: my father joined the Army; his brother Gene, the Navy; and his brother Jack, the Coast Guard.

My father was smart and capable, but he was also stubborn, unpredictable, and explosive. Given his rebellious nature (and thereby inherent problem with figures of authority), he and the Army had quite the oil-and-water relationship. The yoke of "the curse of the Irish" – the strongly-rumored connection between Irishmen and alcohol – had also come to weigh heavily about his neck around the time he enlisted. The demon rum had simultaneously become his best friend and his worst enemy. It fueled the dark side of his nature, creating a true Dr. Jekyll and Mr. Hyde persona and, thus, contributing to disciplinary issues throughout his service.

After basic training my father became a medic. He was later stationed in the Pacific theater as a surgical assistant. While there he treated countless wounded, including those whose bodies bore witness to the inhumane torture inflicted upon them by the enemy. The stories shared by the anguished wounded only bolstered his view of the Japanese as subhuman. My father himself was nearly killed when a 500-pound bomb was dropped outside a clearly marked Red Cross tent; that bomb left him with his life but claimed his eardrums. Though he survived the fighting in New Guinea, he developed a lifelong hatred for the Japanese.

He returned from the Pacific at war's end with the throngs of young men older than their years – all grateful to be alive and seeking a more peaceful life. Malaria, yellow fever, a variety of other tropical diseases, and severe inner ear infections had all left their mark and would remain his eternal companions. Upon his return home the curse of drink once again took hold of my father with a vengeance. Alcohol had been the impetus for numerous disciplinary hearings over the years; and so now, despite his three years of service, he was honorably discharged as a private E-1, the same rank he had been designated when he first entered the Army.

The war had been a great victory for the United States and its allies; but, amidst all of our celebrations, homecomings, and national sense of relief at the war's end, there was the realization of the true cost of conflict. That cost was not confined to the money spent for the tools of waging war or to the consequent loss of lives and scarred bodies. The cost of war extended significantly past the physical, to injuries of conscience and perceptions of normalcy. After several years away from home it was challenging for a soldier to regain his place in his family and in the framework of society. For many, the veneer of humanity had slowly worn away, exposing the darker side of our species. The buildings, the economies, and the environment would all recover from the devastation of the war far more quickly than the souls of the men who stood eyewitness. Those men rode the wave of victory home only to find themselves washed ashore on their own personal deserted islands.

And so it was for my father, home from the war with pieces of his soul left in the jungles of New Guinea. His sense of normalcy had to be reestablished in the civilized world to which he returned. He had to figure out how to remove the prosthetic behavioral callus he had developed compliments of the war. The cursed yoke of the drink took its strongest hold yet; alcohol became his choice of treatment for whatever ailed him (whether real or imagined). Obviously, the medicinal effects of the alcohol only brought about temporary relief; once subsided, he would self-medicate with even larger doses to numb his ever-worsening symptoms. His personal battles were yet to be won.

The war was over, and the cities and towns across the country were filled with returning servicemen. Good fortune brought my father to a chance encounter with the woman who would be the best thing that ever happened to him – my mother, Anna McMullen. It was Christmas Eve in New York City. Anna and her best friend had left work early for the day and headed to a bar that was on their way to the subway station. The bar was loud, smoke-filled, and crowded with people who were already celebrating the holiday. A tall, slender, redheaded young Irishman approached Anna by chance. As my mother recalls, his opening line was "I like your hat." In those days it seemed that everyone (men and women alike) wore a hat. They struck up a conversation. My mother, always street-smart, felt at ease with this entertaining young gentleman. He shared with her the fact that he was in the area shopping for a gift for his mother: a set of silver rosary beads which he had found at a nearby jewelry shop. Seeing the gift herself insured his story's legitimacy; and so they had a few drinks and continued to talk for some time. When my mother was ready to leave, my father asked if he could escort her home. Comfortable with her new acquaintance, she cordially agreed. Thus began the courtship of Mike Moynihan and Anna McMullen.

Although it would seem out of character to those who knew him, my father was a romantic of the old school when it came to their courtship. One day while I was having a cup of tea with my mother, she shared the story about their second encounter. As she explained, it was only a week after their initial meeting at the bar. She and her friend were leaving the linoleum factory where they worked on 31st Street in Manhattan one afternoon when, lo and behold, they saw my father outside the building behind the reins of a splendid horse-drawn carriage that he had commandeered from his father's business in Central Park. He greeted them in a gentlemanly fashion and offered them a ride to their next destination. All dressed up and sporting a top hat, he made quite an impression.

After loading the ladies into the carriage, he sped off, throwing both of them back in their seats as he demonstrated his finest horsemanship. Handling a carriage on the busy streets of New York City required skill and undivided attention; and so it was more than a little disconcerting when they realized that he was terribly drunk. He raced through the streets at a speed far too fast for even the casual observer. Forced to brake hard for building traffic, he came to a sudden stop before deciding to advance around the stopped cars by climbing the curb. The carriage jolted wildly as the wheels rose onto the sidewalk, bouncing the two passengers he sought to impress back and forth. White-knuckled and holding on for dear life as they trotted past shocked pedestrians, my mother and her friend couldn't wait for the ride to be over. Upon reaching the next corner, the carriage bounced over the curb; and my father proceeded to cross the street back onto the next sidewalk. After that second block, traffic had cleared enough to return to the street. My father continued at a dizzying, unsafe pace until they reached the train station on 10th Avenue. Before he had the chance to turn around to ask my mother, "How did you like that?" she and her friend had already jumped from the carriage. Shaken by the adventurous ride, they yelled, "Thanks!" and quickly disappeared into the subway entrance. My father, undaunted by her abrupt departure that afternoon, pursued his courtship and eventually won the hand of Anna McMullen.

**

I have to wonder what it is that we seek out in a relationship. *Happiness? Wealth? Societal conformity? Sex? Beauty? Companionship?* Perhaps each of these things has a place in our search for a mate. We all stand on the world stage dressed in our earthly persona with cloaks and countenances that project some inner essence. Our performance is one of a lifetime. *Do we truly seek each other out, or is our mate already cast from amidst the characters with whom we interact? Are we positioned by life on stage in such a way that we are destined to perform together as part of some predetermined script? Are we foolish to believe that these choices we make are, in fact, our own?* So much chance, so much coincidence, so much certainty surrounds us as we give way to the question of fate.

Manhattan, New York
Late 1920's

I received a call from my mother in 1996 after she finished reading the newly-released book by Frank McCourt, *Angela's Ashes.* "You have to read this book. It's about the trials of an Irish family ravished by poverty and alcoholism." After a brief pause, she said, "I felt like I was reading the story of my own childhood." Then she cried.

My mother had a tough childhood, indeed, but she was a survivor. She was endowed with an indomitable positive spirit that would enable her to weather the toughest of challenges throughout her life. She would say, "When times are hard, you need to take joy in the simplest of things." My mother's greatest quality had to have been her remarkable capacity for forgiveness. The trials inherent to her life – the pain, the disappointment, and the poverty – would never find a permanent place to dwell upon her smiling face. She would only ever radiate warmth, kindness, love, and understanding.

Born to Joseph and Johanna McMullen in 1925, my mother was the oldest of five children. She was born in a taxi crossing midtown Manhattan on the way to the hospital. An inauspicious arrival, it was certainly a bad omen of things to come for this newest addition to a poor, troubled immigrant family. The McMullen's first born, John, had passed away some years earlier from diphtheria; he was only two years old. The early deaths of young children were not uncommon at that time, especially for those recent immigrants living in poverty.

Like most immigrant families of that time, they found housing in a poor neighborhood (a slum) of the Bronx, at the northern tip of Manhattan. Times were tough for the McMullen family. My grandmother found work from time to time, but my grandfather had trouble both finding and keeping work due to his chronic drinking. The cursed drink drained the little money they had and did nothing to help maintain a stable lifestyle for the family of seven. Poverty was so widespread at that time. The few social services available came largely through the Catholic Church. Government help was advanced only to the poorest of the poor; but, although they reluctantly qualified, it wasn't enough.

The physical and emotional pains of poverty and alcohol pushed down upon the McMullen's as they struggled in what seemed to be a losing battle. They could only press on and deal with life as it came each day. Forgetting the hunger and emotional upset of yesterday and avoiding the thought of what tomorrow might bring, they focused on what needed to be done to survive each present day. Disappointment, ridicule, anger, and desperation were their constant companions. My young mother's family was always trying to seek out the sunshine and rise above the clouds of a life filled with uncertainty. They were always one step from eviction and the bill collector. The proverbial "wolf at the door" did not just knock; he had invited himself in and taken up residency.

My mom described my grandmother as a bitter woman disheartened with life. Apparently, she could only find solace in a bottle of Mrs. Applebaum's snake oil (at $0.25 per pint). My mother had the job of procuring the elixir. One time she was followed to Mrs. Applebaum's by an investigator from Social Services who later showed up at the house to inquire about her parents' excessive drinking. While her mother denied that any drinking was going on in their house, her youngest brother, Jimmy, pulled back the curtain under their sink to show the investigator all the empty bottles.

Despite the scrutiny by Social Services, they found it much easier to buy bootleg drink than to make it themselves. My grandfather had previously tried his own hand at distillery and failed. My mother once told me that he woke up the whole house one morning, screaming at the top of his lungs, "Oh my God, Oh my God!" as if the world was ending. A barrel of mash that he had been brewing in the kitchen had spilled out during the night. Being that it was winter in a cold water flat, the resulting spill had turned into a rotten-smelling slush that flowed throughout the apartment. It was a disgusting mess, and that horrible smell lingered long after it was cleaned up.

It was hard to believe that their life could get much worse...but then the stock market crashed in 1929, ushering in a national financial tragedy. My mother was only five years old at the time. At an age when most kids were playing with dolls, she was lucky if her family had food to eat. Their struggle became more intense, but they managed to push on year after dreadful year, finding survival a matter of self-determination. Helped at times by the church, relatives, or the city, each day behind them was a victory possibly bringing them one day closer to better times.

Living in a stalemate of poverty and poor health for years, my grandmother contracted tuberculosis. A disease rarely seen today, tuberculosis took many a malnourished life in those times. She was admitted to a facility in New York City reserved for the isolation and rehabilitation of TB patients. Given her father's inability to run the household, my mother, at the young age of 14, became the *de facto* head of the family. A great responsibility for her age, she sought to maintain some semblance of normalcy for her siblings while their mother recovered in the hospital. Sadly, as fate would have it, Johanna McMullen succumbed to the effects of her illness and passed away in the winter of 1939. Years later my mother described her passing in terms of her just giving up on life; the disappointments, the struggles, and the hopelessness had simply eroded her desire to live. With a weakened body to accompany her weakened spirit, she slipped from this life, leaving behind yet one more trauma for the young family to endure.

My mother and her siblings did whatever they could to help make ends meet beyond what they received through charity. They all took on odd jobs: delivering papers, shining shoes, anything to make a few pennies. The humiliation of being on the dole (as it was called) had long since abated to the need to survive. Then came the dreaded knock on the door of their 137th Street apartment. They all knew who it was as they had been anxiously anticipating his arrival for some time; it was the inspector from the child advocates' agency. Some days before his arrival they had received a letter announcing the need for a review of their family's living conditions. It appeared that a concerned neighbor had reported their situation to the authorities; but, in fact, it was the result of my mother taking matters into her own hands. At a young 14 years of age, she was wise enough to see that the family needed help for their worsening state of affairs.

Some time prior to this fateful day she had made her way to the offices of New York City Social Services and sought out a caseworker to whom she described her family's living conditions. Just another example of how bad things were during the Depression, the caseworker was not very surprised by their story despite how bad it was. She inquired as to whether or not there was any physical or sexual abuse taking place. My mother was shocked by the question and responded, "No, nothing of the sort." Then she asked my mother if their father was bringing home strange women. "No. He's just drunk all the time and can never hold a job. My mother just died in the hospital from TB. My two sisters and younger brother have whooping cough. We have no money for food or clothes, and we are always getting evicted." Having laid out her case to the best of her ability, my mother was told that someone would be looking into their situation. She left the office knowing that a caseworker would soon be coming to inspect their home.

While her father answered the door, my mother organized everyone to stay busy: sweeping the floor, polishing, doing whatever they could to make a good impression. She had also ensured everyone's face and hands were washed. It was clear that the child advocate was immediately upset by what he saw: a drunken Irishman answering the door in a rundown apartment filled with five motherless, skinny, malnourished kids. My mother noticed that the advocate was near tears after examining their living quarters and speaking with her father and siblings; such was the striking condition of things.

While examining the bedrooms, the advocate had asked where the mattresses were; her father's answer painted a self-portrait of insanity. My grandfather's story serves as a clear example of how there is no way to truly understand the behavior of the addicted. Bizarre, unpredictable, and unforgivable, an alcoholic will do almost anything to get to that next drink. One day after returning home from school, my mother found her father "three sheets to the wind" – drunk as could be. How he got money for whiskey was a mystery to my mother...until she entered her bedroom to discover there was no mattress on her bed. Not only was her mattress gone, but so were the rest of the mattresses in the house. Her father, in a moment of desperation for a drink, had found something he could sell: their mattresses. It was a sad situation. If the money from the sale had been used for food – or anything else besides whiskey to quell his habit – it would have been understandable. Just to picture him hauling his children's mattresses – one of the few basic comforts they had – down three flights of stairs and then trying to sell them in the street, was heartbreaking. *Who in their right mind sells their children's mattresses?* To replace them would be difficult, if not impossible; and then there would always be the worry of whether or not he would sell them again.

There were other untold stories about things being sold by their father to get money for whiskey. On one occasion my mother heard a great commotion coming from inside as she approached their apartment. There was screaming and the crashing of furniture. She could hear her younger brother, Joseph, yelling, "I'm going to kill you." Frantically entering the apartment she saw her brother with one hand around her father's throat and the other holding a baseball bat above his head, threatening his life. While trying to separate them, the reason for her brother's rage emerged. Joseph was a hard worker who had struggled for months, earning pennies at a time doing odd jobs and errands, to save up enough money to buy a new winter jacket. Having finally accomplished his goal and proud of what he had achieved, he had returned home that afternoon only to discover his father had sold that hard-earned new jacket for whiskey.

The mattress story alone was enough to render the inspector speechless. Shortly after his visit the family's situation grew further complicated; my mother's sister Kathleen was diagnosed with tuberculosis and removed from the home. It was soon determined that the McMullen children – Anna, Joseph, James, and Mary – would be sent to St. Joseph's Home for Destitute Children on the Hudson River in Poughkeepsie, New York. Kathleen would join them once she had recovered from TB.

The children were all shocked and worried about the move, but they also understood it would bring some relief from their troubled circumstances. At least they would all be going to the same place. After packing the few belongings they possessed into boxes, they loaded them into the car that would transport them to Poughkeepsie. None of the children had ever traveled outside of the city; so, despite their apprehension, the car ride up the Hudson River was an exciting experience. When they arrived at the gates of the institution, they were all filled with fear of what might come next. The driver announced, "This is it." They traveled up a long, winding driveway that divided the facilities. The trees and lawns that blanketed the grounds were in sharp contrast to the poor city neighborhoods they had called home. They gathered up their belongings and exited the car, tears filling their eyes as the reality of their situation manifested before them. Having been pulled from their home, as dismal as it was, they were now being ushered into another world where they would be, for all purposes, orphans. Ultimately, though, my mother and her siblings knew they would now share a better life with children of similar circumstance. Together they would be sheltered, fed, educated, disciplined, and, most importantly, cared for here at St. Joseph's. Having been removed from their homes, their parents, and their respective troubling conditions, many of the children of that generation were being forced to mature early – it was a quick and certain maturity that would soon be tested by World War II, looming closely on the international horizon.

Huddled together and moving as one, with my mother at the center, they were greeted by a smiling nun. Sister Victoria asked, "Are you the McMullen's?" Her pleasant disposition helped to ease their shared anxiety. My mother recalled that they were given a number by Sister Victoria when they first entered the orphanage. Her number was 42; it was a number she would never forget. Nor would she ever forget Sister Victoria, a woman who provided her simple kindness at a time when she needed it most. There would be no visits from their father during their years at the orphanage, only a few from his sister, their aunt, Annie.

The Catholic Church, with its numerous facilities supported by church parishes, was instrumental in supplementing the limited and overburdened social services that existed during the Depression. St. Joseph's Home for Destitute Children was run by Catholic nuns. It was a hard place to endure, but proved no harder than the slum that had previously been their home. In some ways life at the orphanage was much easier. Checked for lice, given physical exams, and provided clean clothes, they had found a comparatively better life. The uncertainty of where their next meal would come from or whether their father would be on a drunken bender were replaced by the security of regular meals, a sense of structure and discipline, and the ever-watchful eyes of the nuns who seemed to be everywhere, omniscient and powerful in their role as surrogate parents.

After two years my mother, then 17, was granted release from the home into the care of her aunt, Annie. She promised her brothers and sisters that she would do her best to get them out as soon as she could. Annie provided my mother with a place to live and whatever comforts she could, given her own modest living conditions. She was so different from her brother and sought, it would seem, to make up for his deficiencies as a father. My mother referred to her aunt as "the white-haired angel," always ready to lend a helping hand when things got bad, providing some bit of food or just a few dollars for survival.

The attack on Pearl Harbor soon changed everyone's life: men were entering the service in droves, creating job opportunities across the nation for the unemployed. My mother, having promised to bring her siblings back from St. Joseph's Home for Destitute Children, put her high school education on hold so that she could work to raise enough money to get an apartment and support them. Oh how my mother hated the name of that place. St. Joseph's Home or St. Joseph's Orphanage would have been fine, but to be labeled "destitute" was disheartening – demoralizing, in fact. While applying for jobs she couldn't help but feel that many opportunities were lost by having to state that her high school and residence for the last few years had been in a home for the "destitute" – that word simply did not conjure up a favorable picture of those whom it represented. When she finally did secure work, she worked hard. My mother managed to get an apartment and, one by one, brought her brothers and sisters back into society. Years later, owning a home would be very important to her as that home would provide the sense of permanence – the stability – that was so lacking in her childhood.

Staten Island, New York
Late 1960's

Under a constant state of renovation for several years, our home on Richmond Road was really starting to take shape. We discovered the house offered more space than we could ever use ourselves. There was a two-bedroom apartment on the second floor; and so my family decided to open our door to my father's mother and her two sisters, Mini and Nora. Since the death of my grandfather a few years earlier, all three sisters had been living together in a declining Manhattan neighborhood that had recently become quite dangerous. Also, as they were all well up in their 80's and 90's, they could use some assistance with their daily living needs. There was even some speculation that the forgetfulness they were each experiencing could have been the early stages of Alzheimer's disease.

Once the apartment was readied, they moved in without much fanfare. These three sisters, all Irish immigrants, were an interesting addition to our already busy lifestyle. My grandmother, Hannah, was the matriarch of the Moynihan family. She wasn't the warmest of grandmas, but she was quick to offer a cup of tea and some tea crackers whenever we came into the apartment. As she was always very "proper," this seemed a fitting formality. She seemed content to share the remaining years of her life together with her sisters. She played the concertina, a small hand-held accordion akin to a music box. Every so often we would coax her to play. She would pick it up from the fireplace mantle; and, with a joyful reluctance, she would belt out the very same Irish tune every time, all the while dancing around the room. She had probably played that song a thousand times before; it was a song she learned from her family as a child. Nora and Mini would laugh with delight as she played. The concertina's music seemed to bring them back to their childhoods, when they would pass their nights sitting around a sod-filled hearth, entertaining themselves simply with song and music. Their eyes would sparkle and a trace of nostalgia would accompany their smiles as they clapped and sang, amplifying their Irish brogues all the more. Whenever I witnessed my grandmother playing her concertina, I couldn't help but feel how out of character it was for her to be performing; yet her revelry was contagious, and we would often be compelled to join in their simple, spirited celebrations.

At first these grand old ladies were not a great burden, but after some months passed they required more and more attention. Doctor visits, medications, falls, and strange incidents began to occur – in an odd way all three seemed to be suffering from forgetfulness and disorientation. My mother was a great caregiver. She was always attentive to their needs and kept a watchful eye on their diets, bills, and medications. We all helped where we could. I remember going to a local drugstore for them on one occasion; the list of things to buy included 6 quarts of milk of magnesia. I remember, at 13 years old, being embarrassed when asking for the large amount of the liquid antacid. The pharmacist laughed as he asked, "Why so much? Are you having a party?" I don't know what they were doing, but those ladies sure consumed a lot of that stuff.

As the days passed, the sisters' collective memory loss seemed to accelerate quickly, as did the number of concerning incidents that ensued. One morning a knock at the door brought us face-to-face with a policeman escorting my grandmother in her nightgown, carrying a purse and wearing her ever-present pearl necklace. Apparently, a concerned neighbor had noticed her wandering around the neighborhood and called the cops. Indignant toward her unrequested escort, she turned from the cop and said, "I know exactly where I'm going, thank you very much." Her wanderings became so frequent that we had to keep a constant eye on her.

I realized that growing old could be a tough process. There were many changes to deal with, both mentally and physically, once youth and middle age became distant experiences. Living as a senior citizen brings about a decline in so many of the strengths that we take for granted – including those traits and memories that make us who we are. Like a tree losing its leaves in autumn, I watched as the sisters' memories broke free from the branches of their minds, disappearing upon the winds of time, never to be known again. The precious, the painful, the joyous, and the difficult impressions somehow stored in our minds were clearly ephemeral in nature. Before my very eyes I could see the portraits of their lifetimes, the mental records of their waking days, simply fading away. These three sisters were so intimately connected. They had shared almost a century of life together, and now they relied on one another to maintain a connection to that life, to a past that was becoming more elusive with each passing day. As I watched them all slowly slipping away, I came to realize that life may be brief, and so we need to make it meaningful – to celebrate, recognize, and claim our place in this, our allotted time, before we, too, are gone.

One night I awoke from a sound sleep to find, to my horror, that there was someone standing at the foot of my bed. I could only see a silhouette. Now around that time there had been a number of burglaries in our neighborhood, so I immediately decided that the burglar was here with me in my room...with God knows what intention. Scared to death, I quietly and slowly reached over to my bookshelf to grab my Boy Scout knife. Opening it, and preparing myself for the worst, I decided I would jump from my bed, throw on the light, and confront the intruder. My heart pounding in my chest, I sprang from the bed, knife in hand and ready to strike. Once I turned on the lights, I was shocked to see my grandmother standing there in her nightgown. Her hair was in a wild state, and her eyes kept a fixed stare. She turned to look at me and said, "There are six men under my bed, and they are big." I called out in my best *we got a problem here* voice: "Hey mom, you better come up here." My parents arrived quickly and escorted my grandmother back to her bed, assuring her all the while that there was no one under her bed or anywhere else in her room. It was quite a bizarre experience to find myself wielding a knife with murderous intent in front of my grandmother in the middle of the night. As shocked as I was, I was relieved it was not that burglar after all. I wouldn't be the only one in our house to have an unexpected visitor pay a surprise mid-night visit.

"Anna! Mike! Wake up!" The startling call came from Nora, standing at the foot of my parents' bed some weeks later. My father yelled, "What the hell's going on?" Nora promptly told him: "Hannah is trying to kill Mini!"

Nora was so scared that she relieved herself right there before my parents could even respond. Quickly running upstairs, they found my grandmother pouring a can of talcum powder over Mini's head and then threatening her with the can. Powder was flying everywhere. My mother grabbed the fragrant weapon and asked what she was doing. My grandmother replied that Mini would not let her go home to Ireland. Mini (93 years old and all of 80 pounds) was quite the sight, a nervous wreck covered in powder, all the while pleading with her sister: "Han, Han, what are you doing? You are not making any sense!" My mother, an expert at defusing difficult situations, told Hannah that she would personally take her home to Ireland; but, because it was a long trip, they should have a proper meal and a cup of tea first. Once in the kitchen, my mother started making bacon and eggs; she managed to incorporate one of my grandmother's sleeping pills into the meal. Though still insistent on returning to Ireland, my grandmother finally began to calm down a little. After a short repast, a proper cup of tea, and a little small talk, she was ready for bed. Her trip home to Ireland was successfully postponed.

By then I was up from bed and had joined the fray – what a scene! As always, my mother seemed to have things under control. My grandmother was calming down. Nora was walking around in circles, wet from having peed her pants; my mother suggested that she should go change her clothes. We began helping poor Mini dust off the powder that covered her head and dress; she was really a mess, and truly upset by her sister's unexpected behavior. Mini's eyesight was very bad, and the thick lenses of her glasses distorted the beauty of her troubled, smiling blue eyes. She struggled to clear the powder from her glasses, nervously rubbing them with her dress, all the while thanking my mother for her help: "I don't know what we would do without you."

Amidst all the drama there were some lighter moments with the sisters. At the age of 89, Nora was the youngest. She made regular trips to the bathroom down the hallway past our room at night, carrying a bedpan that sloshed as she inched her way ever so slowly down the hall. When she reached our room, she would always peer in before moving on; it was a habit that we felt to be somewhat intrusive. One night, around Halloween, my brother decided to give Nora a little surprise the next time she stuck her head in the door. Fred's bed was right next to the door. He had a big, grotesque-looking rubber hand that he put on his foot. He planned to pull the covers up toward his head and reveal the shocking hand when Nora peered in. That night, as Nora was heading down the hall, we both laughed quietly under our covers in anticipation of what was to come. Sure enough, as soon as her head popped in the door, Fred sprang into action, pulling the covers off his prop and giving it a good shake. Nora screamed and, as she quickly shuffled down the hall, the cargo in her bedpan breached its sides, making quite a mess. We caught hell for scaring her, but our recollection of the childish prank brought us laughter for many years to come.

Over time my grandmother's condition worsened to a point where we could no longer give her the care or the attention that she needed. We were always concerned that she might hurt herself or her sisters; or, God forbid, start a fire while cooking. Most of her events (as we would call them) seemed to occur in the middle of the night. On one occasion I woke up around 4:00 a.m. to the sound of rock 'n roll music blasting from their apartment. Surprised by the hour, the volume, and the type of music playing, I went up to their living room only to find them sitting in their chairs having a cup of tea. "Hey, what's going on?" I asked. They looked at me, surprised, and said, "Nothing. Nothing is going on." I told them it was four o'clock in the morning, but they insisted, "Oh no, it's four in the afternoon." Now it was winter, and so the sun did disappear early; but they would not hear it. Their internal clocks were out of whack, and, try as I might, I could not convince them of the true time. Even Mini, the most clear-minded of the three, seemed unaware of what was happening. She looked frail, but she had her wits about her. She always seemed upset by the slow deterioration of her sisters' faculties, often kindly correcting them when they said or did something inappropriate; but she was just as confused this time. Finally, I told them, "I hope you don't mind, but I'm going to turn the music down just a little." With that, I bid them good night and went back to bed.

After numerous such events, and several doctor and hospital visits, my father (in agreement with his brothers and sister) decided that my grandmother should be placed in a nursing home. She had been diagnosed with arteriosclerosis and a host of other ailments that commonly plagued those whose age drew close to the century mark. I could see that my father and his siblings struggled in making this heartbreaking, but necessary decision. They had agonized over what should be done and, in the end, had chosen the only real option available. Although in her best interest, it was a hard task. To commit someone you love to a nursing home – to take them away from everything familiar, to entrust them to strangers, and to assure them that everything would be okay as they pleaded not to go – takes incredible strength.

Once in the nursing home where she would spend her final days, my grandmother's health slowly declined. She passed away. Nora and Mini followed soon after in shocking succession.

The sisters had moved through this life together, sharing one another's joys and sorrows; and so it seemed fitting that they continued their journey into their next life in close step. Their passing left a large void in our home.

***

The void left by the sisters' passing was soon filled by another relative, my mother's youngest brother, Jimmy. He had been the last of my mother's siblings to leave St. Joseph's home and join them in their New York City apartment. He made his way into society and married early. Then, at the age of 17, he joined the Navy. Barely able to meet the weight requirements, he reportedly consumed a large volume of bananas before being weighed in. He shipped out to sea on a six-month cruise, leaving behind a pregnant wife with instructions to contact my mother whenever she needed help. Jimmy McMullen obviously had no idea of the responsibilities of having a family. He struggled with a failed marriage; and along the way, the curse of the Irish that had plagued his now-departed father, quietly crept into his life as well. Alcohol became Jimmy's closest friend, his confidant, his love. His father was accompanied to his grave by his obsession with drink; like so many souls before him, death had proven the only escape from that lifelong bond.

Jimmy had lived with us on and off over the years while he was serving in the Navy. In those days we were still in the projects and didn't have a lot of room, but when it came to family we always seemed to make space. Now we had more space than we needed; and so Jimmy took up permanent residence with us. He would live on the first floor of our house, in an apartment that we had finally finished after an extensive renovation. He joined us each night for dinner. My mother washed his clothes and tended to his needs as she had so many years ago when they were children. Quiet and reserved by nature, he usually kept to himself...unless he was loaded, and then he became the life of the party, a comedian and a hell-raiser – a totally different person.

The weekends were Jimmy's downfall. Employed as a steelworker alongside my father, he was making a good living.

He discovered some local watering holes where he felt comfortable and would gravitate to them beginning every Friday night. Through the course of the weekends' two nights he would blow his entire paycheck on booze, always buying rounds of drinks for his fellow patrons. He would typically return home staggering drunk, sometimes bearing wounds from barroom fights or falls from a barstool.

I always felt sorry for my Uncle Jimmy. There was a sadness that seemed to surround him, a weight that he carried – a burden no one else could share. In quiet moments sitting across from him at our kitchen table, smoke rising from his ever-present cigarette and a cup of coffee in his hand as he stared off at nothing in particular, I could sometimes see the depth of his despair.

My father was always fond of quoting Thoreau, a 19th century writer, philosopher, and naturalist. His favorite quote seemed to best characterize Jimmy: "Most men lead lives of quiet desperation." I think my father's fondness for this particular quote resulted from how it also unknowingly captured the world in which he lived. Ironically, he was also a prime example of Thoreau's words; quiet desperation was clearly his default state of mind. I would gain greater insight into the meaning of that quote myself in future years, during my tour as an infantryman in Vietnam. It expressed the nature of most men in the course of their lives. Faced with the challenges of our time on this earth, most of us are forced to endure circumstances and lifestyles not of our own choosing, but rather dictated by fate. Powerless in many instances to change our circumstances, we are left to endure, often quietly, what life brings our way. Despite our aspirations, dreams, endeavors, and predictions of what could be, most of us are left desperately trying to make life work – to grasp some happiness, accomplishment, recognition, and peace – and to contribute something back into society so as not to be forgotten.

In my experience, there certainly did appear to be a strange connection between Irishmen and alcohol – it seemed more often than not to target us for companionship. And I think that every one of my relatives who experienced some problem with drinking was prompted to either to dance or fight. In Jimmy's case, he was a dancer, and alcohol played the tunes. If by some chance he was at home while drunk, he would become very outspoken, putting aside his usual quiet demeanor to join us in the kitchen for some brief socialization. At times he would get up from the table and break into a spirited dance session – with or without music – performing only for himself like a whirling dervish in the midst of an alcoholic trance. He would flail around like a scarecrow on fire, working his skinny frame through the large kitchen, usually avoiding obstacles. Occasionally he would fall to the floor only to rise unshaken, laughing wildly until he could no longer breathe. All the while, he would be reaching for his ever-present cigarette that burned in the ashtray atop the table. His uncharacteristic behavior made him appear to be out of his mind; yet we shamelessly tended to encourage his insanity, clapping and cheering him on as he worked himself into a frenzy. Those flights from reality typically brought us all to laughter. Our entertainment usually came to an end when Jimmy was summoned to the curb by a taxi, alerting him of its arrival with a series of honks. He would always yell out, to no one in particular, "Hey, your horn works. Now try your brakes!" With that, he would be off to do his circuit of local bars. Even though his drunken behavior would make us laugh wildly, we were thankful he never got a license to drive.

His life changed very little as the years passed. Jimmy seemed content with his way of navigating this world: he worked, ate, watched TV, slept, and was drunk every weekend (and, sometimes, a couple of nights during the week). There were no romantic encounters as he had but one true love, alcohol.

There was one occasion, however, when I saw him come back to life. His daughter (from his marriage that ended long ago) contacted him; at the age of 19, she wanted to meet her father. Like so many children who have grown up in the absence of a parent, she wanted to meet her flesh and blood, the contributor to her existence. She was full of the questions that haunt the minds of those who grow up in the absence of a parent in a family divided. As there had been no interaction between them for all those years, Jimmy was startled at first by the request to reconnect with his child. He was obviously nervous about their reunion, but he set up a time for her to come to our home on Staten Island. In the time that passed before their meeting, his drinking seemed to come to a sudden halt. He put his typical lifestyle – his routine, his best friend, his true love – on hold.

The Saturday of his daughter's arrival found him spruced up, clean-shaven with an extra dose of All Spice aftershave and, above all, sober. We were all present in support of Jimmy's difficult meeting. We also wanted to meet his daughter, the cousin we never knew existed. She arrived with a friend and a half-sister. An attractive young lady with a warm and winning smile, Joanna was immediately recognizable as Jimmy's daughter. Introductions and hugs ensued. I could see Jimmy beaming with pride through his nervousness. We all talked at lunch and then strolled around in the yard; it was a pleasant visit. Jimmy and Joanna were able to spend some time alone to discuss those private matters that brought her to seek him out. Some hours later we all got further acquainted over dinner. The girls headed home with promises of another visit, but that reunion would never come to be.

Jimmy's childhood – or lack thereof – could certainly account for his broken connection with his daughter. Fortunate are those who have not experienced the saddening division of their family. The all-too-frequent painful separation of families creates a void that is difficult to fill but easy to perpetuate. True, surrogates can provide a family structure and offer care, but somehow that sense of family is never quite the same as being with one's own blood. However brief their reunion, it served to heal their long-open, shared wounds of separation. Their embrace, some kind words, and a few smiles in their short time together that afternoon had proven incredibly meaningful.

Shortly after the visit from his daughter, Jimmy went back to his former lifestyle. As his drinking increased, his health (which had been pretty good through the years) began to worsen. He was diagnosed with pancreatitis, a devastating disease directly related to alcohol consumption. Alcohol was, indeed, a curse. The doctor told Jimmy to stop drinking completely as introducing even the smallest amount of alcohol would accelerate the disease and cause extreme pain. However, as with most people who receive this diagnosis, he would feel a little better and then try to drink, only to be overcome with the distress that would inevitably result from any pancreatic transgression. Alcohol punishes the sick alcoholic in the most painful of ways when they give in further to their addiction.

Sick, in constant pain, losing weight, and, at times, jaundiced, Jimmy struggled through some agonizing months. Then one weekend when everyone was away from home (which never seemed to happen), he became seriously ill. I was the first to return home after having spent the weekend at the Jersey Shore. I found him in his bed – unable to get up, listless, dehydrated, and barely able to speak. He was clearly dying. I picked him up and carried him out of the house to my car. I drove him to a nearby hospital where, after a short time in the emergency room, he was admitted. His condition was critical. After a short battle with pancreatitis, he joined the growing list of casualties from alcohol on July 27, 1974. He was killed by the poison to which he had become addicted in a loving, suicidal relationship. It was sad to see him go; he was only 42 years old.

My cousins and I gathered together the night before Jimmy's funeral; we all got terribly drunk. It was ironic as drinking had brought about his death; yet we felt it was a fitting way to celebrate his life. The next day we made our way to the church and then on to cemetery for a final goodbye. The McMullen siblings were all in attendance to bid farewell to their youngest brother. Jimmy's parting was sad but, given his lifestyle, not surprising. After a troubled life, he was finally free from suffering. The peace that awaits us all was now his.

Coming together in celebration of a lost life with song and drink was a splendid Irish tradition brought to these shores from the old country. There is no better or more fitting reason for one of Irish blood to drink than to honor the passing of a family member. I remember attending wakes as a child in New York City. When we arrived, the men would quickly give their condolences before disappearing to the nearest tavern to warm their souls and raise a glass in celebration of the passing of their blood. Drinking shots and beers eased their pain and facilitated the grieving process. Sometimes, those who had come to pay their respects would get lost in the moment of remembering the dead with song and drink and forget to return to the wake; they were usually pulled from their barstool perches by angry wives humiliated by their drunken spouses' absence from the funeral home. Fights between cousins or brothers over some long-forgotten indiscretions would often accompany these impromptu barstool vigils.

***

Never needing to search for new tenants at 955 Richmond Road, my father's sister, Mary, and her flamboyant husband, Jim Greene, took up residence on our second floor shortly after Jimmy's passing. Mary was my father's older sister. They had what I would describe as a "strained" relationship; they were always at odds with one another (from childhood) but managed to put aside their differences. Mary always seemed to maintain a prudish way about her; she was critical and failed to display any emotion. Her husband was a real character. A closet drinker, he didn't drink in bars but rather chose his home environs for his sessions with John Barleycorn – and unusual sessions they were. On any given night Jim would quickly fall under the spell of the Irish demons that dwelled in his bottles of gin. His antics were predictable and sad, yet comical. He would have conversations with some imaginary figure – full conversations, where he would supply the positions on both sides of whatever debate was on tap for the evening. His ramblings, on just about any topic, were regularly punctuated by his favorite expression: "Pow-wow-wow." We had no idea what it meant. We could hear him in just about any part of the house as he bellowed from upstairs at his kitchen table. We would pick up on those especially loud diatribes and laugh like hell when he really got going. We would even anticipate and mimic his high-volume *wow-wows*. "So you think you're pretty smart, eh? Well you are not as smart as you think you are! Pow-Wow-Wow." Mary would regularly chime in, telling him to be quiet as she tried to register in his inebriated mind; but he would just turn to his imaginary companions and say, "Listen to her. Pow-wow-wow." If we saw him in the morning after a particularly noisy evening, he would act as though nothing out of the ordinary had occurred the night before; but the clanking of the empty gin bottles every time he took out the trash told the story of his not-so-private parties.

On one occasion he happened to be sitting next to an open window in his kitchen during one of his episodes. He was carrying on so loudly that one of our neighbors got concerned and, fearing someone was being threatened, called the police. When the police arrived we tried to convince them that all was well, and that Jim was just having a good time. The cop still went up to check on him, but was quickly satisfied that Jim's bellowing was only between himself and his demons. Mary was humiliated by the police presence. Jim simply let out a more subdued *wow-wow* than usual: "Now the police are here. Big deal. Wow-Wow." After several years of enduring Jim's antics, and after a few heated arguments between my father and his sister, Mary and her husband chose to move on to more accommodating quarters in a housing project.

***

It seemed that our house was continually inhabited by both those actively drinking and those who were actively trying to stop. Our house was a showcase of those who accepted living under a spell and those who sought guidance to freedom.

If you needed help as a recovering alcoholic – especially if you were what my father would call a "hard case" – he was your man. Mean Mike was your way to salvation. He had all the fervor of a Bible-thumping minister; not in a religious sense, but in the ardent way he followed the tenants set forth by Bill W., the founder of AA. If I had to pick a historical figure who reminded me of my father, it would have to be John Brown, a zealous 19th century militant abolitionist hanged before the Civil War for murder and insurrection. The old pictures of John Brown seemed to capture his spirited insanity, the likes of which I could see in my father. Fervent, dedicated, unyielding, and speaking from his own experience, my father would tell people that if they followed the principles put forth by AA, they could beat – though never eliminate – their affliction and carry on normal lives. I can still hear him addressing people in our kitchen in his less-than-sympathetic way from his pulpit that was our kitchen table. His great opening line was "What the fuck is wrong with you?" It was a great way to begin a conversation.

"You think the world owes you something? You think that you're the only son of a bitch with problems? Let me be clear with you, you will not get any sympathy from me. The only (and he would always emphasize the word 'only') problem you have is drinking. Stop feeling sorry for yourself. You are your own worst enemy, so get your shit together. If you want to quit drinking, I'll help you. But I will not put up with any bullshit. You understand me? Do you want another cup of coffee?" That last question was typically his way of returning to a level of civil discussion, allowing his pupil to take a breath and to voice some response after listening to his forceful diatribe.

"I want you to attend seven meetings a week. I'll go with you. I don't want to hear any excuses. These meetings are critical to your sobriety, so get used to them. You will be going to them from now on. I want you to call me every day to see how things are going. For now, the only thing you have to remember – the only thing that you have to do – is not to pick up the first drink."

As hard as he may have been on them, my father was vehemently devoted to his mission of helping people. He was always available to help someone through a hard time – any time of day or night – but he did have his limits. I can remember he once received a call around three o'clock in the morning. Back then the phone woke everyone in the house when it rang. It was one of his pigeons (as he would call those recently under his guidance) calling to tell my father that he was done trying to get sober. His life was a mess, no one understood what he was going through, and he was at his ropes' end. He said he was going to blow his brains out. This was in the days before suicide hotlines. Now my father had no tolerance for self-pity; so he let him go on about how miserable his life was, but when he finally got the opportunity to speak, my father told the shocked alcoholic, "Nice knowing you. Try not to make a big mess." He then hung up the phone and went back to sleep. His philosophy was that if someone was intent upon taking his or her own life, there was nothing anyone could do to prevent it. It angered him when people would use the threat of suicide as a means to garner attention or sympathy. Thankfully, my father was correct in his assumptions, and no one under his guidance ever followed through with the thinly-veiled threats to end their lives.

A universal metaphysician, Mean Mike was never without a remedy for any mental, physical, or spiritual ailment. He always delivered his message with a voice of reassurance and certainty. In fact, he would often tell those people who were concerned about their mental state: "Don't ever worry about being 'crazy' because if you were truly crazy that thought would never enter your mind."

On any given day there would appear at our home those who we would call "the regulars" – those who had been showing up at our kitchen table for years. In accordance with the tradition of AA, we only ever knew them by their first names and last initials. They were an unusual cross-section of humanity, both good and bad, who would stop by for their daily dose of inspiration. Some stood out more than others.

Todd C., a man with the loudest and most annoying voice I have ever heard, had an insatiable desire for coffee and a sixth sense for knowing when our coffee pot was on. He was a chain smoker; I don't think I ever saw him without a cigarette in his hand. He was also truly outspoken; and whether talking about politics, social issues, race, or anything else, he would surely be insulting someone. He reminded me of a modern-day pirate as he cursed frequently and maneuvered on one leg – courtesy of World War II, where his hearing had also been greatly impaired.

Given the fact that he was always popping in unannounced, I had many occasions to engage Todd in conversation around the kitchen table. When you got past his bravado and his volume eased up, he was a truly interesting man. It turned out he was a highly-decorated veteran as the result of a misadventure while fighting the Germans in France. Todd had served in Europe as a forward artillery observer for the Army. His job was to locate German positions and then call in artillery support for Army ground troops. He once discovered a cache of cognac in an abandoned farmhouse while on a reconnaissance patrol in the French countryside. An active alcoholic, he gave in to the temptation of the cache. He became horribly drunk and took a pleasure ride in his jeep, managing to get himself lost as he attempted to return to his headquarters. Driving aimlessly through the woods and farmland, he eventually stopped to relieve himself at the base of a hedgerow. Afterwards, he decided to get a better view of his surroundings, and so he staggered to the top of the hedgerow. To his surprise he discovered a large battery of German artillery. He was shocked that he had not been discovered as he approached the location; somehow he had managed to bypass security. He promptly took out his maps to figure out where he was and radioed headquarters with the German artillery positions. He continued to enjoy the cognac he had discovered earlier until firing began to destroy the enemy artillery. Todd himself adjusted fire onto the position but hastily retreated once he realized how dangerously close he was to the incoming rounds. He made his exit amidst the bombardment and returned to his headquarters a drunken hero. At first he was chastised for his drunken behavior; but then, once the extent of the damage to the enemy was assessed, he was celebrated for his bravery. Based upon this and his other experiences at war, Todd believed a person's fate was preordained. His favorite saying was "If you were meant to be shot, you'll never drown."

The thing I found most remarkable about Todd C. was his ability to remember things he read so clearly that he could not only recount exact passages in books but also cite what pages they were found on. I found his talent truly amazing. He never bragged about his ability and even seemed reluctant to discuss it, as though it were something he felt others would perceive as odd. His gift came to light one evening while he and my father were arguing about some bit of information in a book they had both read. Bristling about being correct, Todd challenged my father to get out the book in question and go to a specific paragraph on a specific page to see who was, in fact, right. Sure enough, Todd was correct. Once his gift had been brought to light, Todd willingly demonstrated his unique talent for us over and over. I was shocked that he possessed such a great gift. Unfortunately, I wasn't shocked that, like so many gifted alcoholic people, Todd was unable to channel his ability into a meaningful part of his life. He may have been intellectually adept, but he was not all that astute: he had significant difficulty making simple decisions and a severe deficiency when it came to participating in the social arena.

South Beach Projects, Staten Island
Late 1950s

My father was brilliant, but he was unusual. A fiery anger that always remained kindled resided within his piercing blue eyes. He was never more than a word, a glance, or a moment away from breaking into a rage. I remember one such occasion vividly. It was a Friday evening in the summertime, around seven o'clock. An impromptu boxing match was underway in a small patch of grass outside our building at 122 Lamport Boulevard in the South Beach projects. The main event was about to begin between my brother Fred and Sammy Larkin, a boy whose apartment was on the first floor right next to where the match was taking place. It was obvious even before the fight began that it was a mismatch. Sammy was much bigger than my brother and known to be much tougher, but my brother was impulsive and chose to take on the challenge. Fred was quickly pummeled after the unexpected punch that started the action. Not that anyone was keeping time, but the fight didn't even seem to reach the three-minute mark to end the first round. It ended quickly with a series of well-placed blows to my brother's head; he assumed a defeated position on the ground. Sammy Larkin's father yelled from his kitchen window, "You two shake hands." Fred, however, having regained his wits and feeling short-changed by the surprise punch that had started the fight, decided to redeem himself. He had slowly gotten to his feet while Sammy was looking toward his father; as Sammy turned back, Fred landed a heavy blow to his chin. Mr. Larkin, enraged, raced out from his apartment. Quickly at ringside, he grabbed my brother by the shoulders and gave him a stern talking to, all the while shaking him for effect. Our father, returning late from work after a stop at the local tavern, happened on the scene at that very moment. He was obviously drunk. "What the fuck are you doing?" *Holy shit,* I thought as my father bellowed, "Get your fucking hands off him!" Mr. Larkin tried to get my father caught up on what had happened, but his effort was to no avail. My father's blood was boiling, and he could not hear a word of the explanation. He roared, "You think you're a tough guy, Larkin? Put the fucking gloves on, you son of a bitch."

And so began the battle royal. A large crowd gathered as the two combatants readied themselves. It was a circus-like atmosphere of perverse entertainment with my father and one of our neighbors at center ring for all to see. Mrs. Larkin put her head out the window to call upon her husband to stop all the nonsense, but he, like my father, had gone deaf to the crowd as he put on his gloves. We kept our distance at first, but morbid curiosity compelled us to gradually move closer. Fighting was (or at least seemed to be) more common back then. You had to "man up," it was the unspoken rule of the time; even if you knew you would lose a fight, you had to take your lumps. My father would say that just as long as you got in one good punch, your opponent would remember who he was fighting for as long as his injury throbbed. That seemed to make sense...unless you ended up throbbing a lot longer than your opponent. All the neighbors were gathering at their windows, and mothers were pulling in their young children so as not to witness the violence to come. The fight began in an almost *civilized* manner. These two working-class fathers seemed to be evenly matched. As the bout commenced, each managed to land some initial head-snapping blows. The contest went back and forth. Blood was apparent on each of their faces as simultaneous cheers and groans arose from the crowd. Each father did his best, bobbing and weaving as they moved around their imaginary ring.

I remember as I watched this spectacle that I was worried someone would get really hurt. I was only nine years old; and so watching my father in a fight with one of our neighbors – creating a long-to-be-remembered scene in front of our whole neighborhood – was both frightening and humiliating at the same time. What I feared most was that the fight might escalate to a point where the gloves would come off, and they would enter into an all-out, no rules brawl. As the fight went on, I could see my father was mad but not quite yet in the state of rage. I could always tell by looking at his eyes – they spoke to his true state of mind. I had once overheard (as children sometimes do) one of his stories about being in an argument with someone who kept pointing a finger in his face. Apparently, he grabbed the man's hand and nearly bit that finger off, sending him to the hospital.

The fight at hand was going on too long for me. My stomach was in knots. I just kept thinking about the numerous stitches in my father's head and face, and the broken fingers that he had returned home with after prior altercations. Finally, both men reached the limits of their winds and removed their gloves.

Each had landed significant blows to the other; each had drawn blood. The fight came to an end in a draw. Neither participant seemed to gain anything from the fight other than maintaining their honor. The fathers shook hands and encouraged their sons to do the same. I was greatly relieved that it ended as it did. Everyone retreated to their apartments. It really had not been an unusual event here in the projects, but what does one to say to their father after witnessing such a scene: *Good job, you really kicked his ass? That was some left hook?* We made our way into the building and rode the elevator to the sixth floor together in solidarity and silence. I'm still not quite sure what words would have been suitable.

Staten Island, New York
Late 1980's

My father was powerful, frightening, and unpredictable. Even into his later years, his proclivity for fighting endured. One day in his 70's he returned from an AA meeting and recounted for us the story of his drive home. He could have been the poster child for road rage. Apparently, after being cut off on the road, he caught up to the offending vehicle at a traffic light. He came to an abrupt stop, threw his car into park, and exited to confront the other driver. As it turned out, that driver was just about his age and just as crazy. One word led to another, and before long they were fighting the fight of old men in the middle of a busy street. Shortly after the match began, two cops arrived and separated the bruised and bloodied septuagenarians. Despite the cops' presence and their mutual exhaustion, the two old men continued to throw insults at one another, all the while trying to throw a few more punches. Patience wearing thin and traffic building around this bizarre scene, one cop finally announced that he was going to let them fight, and then take whoever won to jail. With that, both combatants had an honorable reason to cease hostilities and their chance encounter ended. I remember my father complaining after the incident that his shins were badly bruised: "I had the old fuck in a headlock, but the guy kept kicking me in the shins. That dirty bastard, I should have kicked his ass." Such was life in my father's later, *quieter* years.

During the 1960s the war in Vietnam occupied the minds of the people in our nation more than anything else. Many of us who watched the conflict escalating on TV would one day, years later, wind up fighting there ourselves. Referred to on most maps of that period as *French Indochina,* Vietnam was just a small strip of land on the South China Sea that had been colonized by the French in the 19th century. Throughout history the country had been under siege or occupied by other countries in Southeast Asia. It was inhabited by a population of agrarians who fought fiercely to protect the homeland of their ancestors against invaders.

As a result of the 1954 Geneva conference, the country was divided into two: North Vietnam and South Vietnam. These two countries continued to fight with one another, sporadically, in a contest of ideologies. The North sought reunification of Vietnam under communist rule and was supported by the Russians and the Chinese. The South leaned more toward a pro-Western form of government and so was supported by the United States and many of its allies. A protracted 10-year guerrilla war that would ultimately devastate the country of Vietnam and cost our forces countless lives commenced around 1963.

As the war in Vietnam escalated, the U.S. government imposed a draft that would enlist young American boys into the ranks of the military for two years' service. At 18 years of age, young men were required to register for the draft and could then expect to receive an invitation from Uncle Sam to report for military service around their 19th birthday. They would then have two weeks to get their lives in order before reporting for basic infantry training and assignment to points unknown; their most likely final destination was Vietnam.

Demonstrations against the war were all too frequent as the war showed an insatiable appetite for the lives of our young men. What we knew of wars past had come by way of news reporters, official military statements, or radio; that information was not often shared in a timely fashion. This war in Vietnam, however, was different: it was the first war brought into the living rooms of citizens through the ever-growing media outlet of television. TV promptly brought all the horror that was war directly into our homes. As if the visual element wasn't a frightening enough dose of reality, there was another daily reminder: the statistics of our casualties. These cumulative totals of both the dead and the wounded served as a morbid display of pain in numbers, offering an even more repulsive reckoning of human suffering.

In that time after high school when our lives were just beginning – while we were looking for jobs or considering higher education – we knew we would soon be confronted by the draft. It was a peculiar feeling, one made all the more real as we witnessed the guys we knew (who were just a little older than us) suddenly finding themselves playing the role of citizen soldiers. Their going-away parties portended our own fate.

My father sat me down at the kitchen table, where all important issues were given review. He looked me in the eyes and said, "Your mother told me you were interested in joining the Army." A year earlier he had a similar discussion with my brother Fred who had, with our father's consent, enlisted in the Marine Corps shortly thereafter. As we now sat talking about my enlistment – which was preferable to me than being drafted – the situation overseas had escalated. The Tet Offensive of 1968 (a period of heavy fighting) had begun. The Marines stationed in the northern provinces of South Vietnam were having a bad time of it in places like Khe Sanh; Fred was there, "knee-deep in shit," as my father put it.

Having himself fought in the jungles of New Guinea during World War II, my father was well-versed in the physical and emotional costs of war. He knew the dangers his sons would be facing. Physically, he had suffered the damaging effects of yellow fever, malaria, severe inner ear infections, and the trauma of concussion. Mentally, he had injuries that were so deeply embedded in his mind that they were unreachable; the pressures and horrors of war had left their indelible imprint on his psyche. It had to be difficult for him to vote in favor of our going to war, especially in consideration of the fact that his view of the legitimacy of this war was mixed. Unsure if our involvement was critical to our national interest, he still supported and respected the decisions of our elected leaders.

Assuming the role of a noble pariah is the lot of those who fight our wars. The endorsement of war by participation is seen by some as an unworthy human endeavor. Others see that endorsement as honorable for standing firm in the face of tyranny and protecting lives and liberty at the expense of a soldier's own well-being. Our predicament, as our race on this earth has demonstrated, is that we dwell either at war or in preparation thereof because of the inherent aggressive nature of man. When rhetoric and diplomacy fail to stop the tyrants of any given time in history, when the words of man cannot dissuade those set on domination, a nation that chooses to survive will fight. The Roman General Vegetius once said, "Let him who desires peace prepare for war." That is the sad but necessary reality of this world. We can hold high the banner of the peacekeepers and welcome them amongst all nations, but the bottom line is this: speak to our highest sensibilities and adhere to truth, but let no man take your life, your home, or your country. When viewing the antiwar demonstrations on TV, my father would repeatedly proclaim, "Who in God's name wants war? If the antiwar crowd had their way during World War II, we would all be speaking German and eating rice noodles."

And so, after a short discussion about the war and my decision to join the Army, my father simply said, "I gave your brother the okay to go last year. If you feel you must go, you have my blessing." My father didn't dwell long on emotion. He told me to be careful and not to try to be a hero. He often said that the only true heroes were the ones who didn't come home, those who gave up their lives as an end to the war. He ended the discussion with a simple "Watch your ass." That was it. Not long after that conversation, I went to see the Army recruiter and joined for two years.

In the time prior to my leaving for the service, I became aware that the curse that afflicted my father, my mother's father, and countless members of our extended family, was also my own. If there is such a thing as the early stage of a curse, I was living it. At one point I came home drunk while everyone was eating dinner and got into an argument my father. That scene resulted in me packing my bags and storming out of the house. The next logical course of action (if only in *my* mind) was for me to head off to the Bahamas. Once there, I managed to get into an altercation with a local Bahamian customs agent – that nearly landed me in jail. It took me about a week to sober up and come to my senses. Returning home I was welcomed back into the house with a simple request from my parents that my attitude "be adjusted to conform to that of normal people." Excessive drinking still seemed to be the order of the day.

As it did with so many alcoholics, alcohol clearly had a dramatic effect on my personality. My normally affable nature turned nasty when I drank. Alcohol took away my inhibitions, my good nature, and my common sense; it brought out my dark side. It brought to the surface the anger and insanity that I had long witnessed in my father. Indeed, Dr. Jekyll and Mr. Hyde were one and the same, and we were undoubtedly related.

I first noticed that I had a quick and short temper early on, while I was still in grammar school. Though I never really thought of myself as a problem child, my behavior was certainly akin to what I had witnessed in my father over the years. My temper was disturbing to those around me as it was so out of character from my normal easy-going nature. I could go from calm to belligerent in a split second if something rubbed me the wrong way. Considering the fact that my father had instilled in us the attitude that we should never let anyone push us around (and that he supported fighting, as it was a common occurrence in those days), I fought on a regular basis. In fact, I fought with just about every boy in my class at St. Sylvester's School. Not that I was tough – I was, in fact, the shortest kid in the class, and I lost most of the time – but I just refused to be pushed around or bullied without putting up a fight. In later years, fueled by alcohol, my angry outbursts became more frequent, predictable, and dangerous. The blackouts I began to experience early on should have been a clear indicator that I was on the highway to Hell.

One such incident occurred at the age of 17 when I was nearly killed by a football player who I should have known better than to tangle with; he was a big guy with a nasty attitude. We had exchanged some words in a bar (that we weren't legally supposed to be in) before "taking it outside." Despite his obvious physical advantage over me, he chose to sucker punch me at the curb. The unexpected punch itself would have been enough to knock me out; but, as luck would have it, my temple hit the pointed edge of the windshield of a convertible before I even hit the curb and collapsed into the street. My friends came to my aid and threw me in the back seat of a car. I was told it took a while before I regained consciousness. With one eye swollen shut, my bleeding face was a series of large bumps. My head pounded, and I couldn't see straight. I could only ask, "What the hell happened?" I had suffered a severe concussion, and it would take me over a week to recover. The next morning my mother woke me up, asking, in a disturbed voice, "What happened to you?" My immediate response, not realizing how I looked or the fact that there was blood all over my pillow, was to say, "Nothing." When I looked in the mirror, I understood her distress. All my father had to say about the incident was "You dopey bastard, that guy could've killed you."

Despite the frequency of my fighting and the fact that far too many situations occurred that could have landed me in grave trouble, I managed to avoid all but one run-in with the law.

Among my many transgressions was a drunken driving incident around the high school football field one early winter morning. At the request of the high school principal, I was brought to the stationhouse by the police. I faced a variety of charges, not the least of which was drunk driving. Good fortune prevailed when my presence at the police station was brought to the attention of the station's captain. He happened to be the father of a good friend of mine, and he was able to persuade the arresting officers to go easy on me. I wound up losing my license and was given a bunch of tickets, but that was the end of it. Unfortunately, my lucky break did little to dampen my growing wild spirit.

Drinking had become a regular part of my daily routine as I joined my buddies at the local tavern nightly for beer and pool. Having arrived at my 18th birthday my consumption was now legal, despite the fact it had been going on for some time. In fact, starting at the age of 14, my friends and I had managed to get our hands on beer at least once a week. We would make our way down to the train overpass to avoid detection, each with a six-pack in tow. We would smoke cigars, drink beer, sing, talk shit to one another, and usually puke before returning home with a mouth full of gum (preferably sen-sen). Our drunkenness seemed to unify us. Underage drinking was frowned upon but never seen as a real big issue; it was just something that kids would do at that time. For us, drinking was a rite of passage: you had to learn how to consume your alcohol, control the resulting altered state, and endure the hangovers that inevitably followed.

***

My good friend Larry Mondello and I enlisted in the Army at the same time. Prior to our becoming the military's problem, we engaged ourselves in a few last wild escapades on the home front. We were a rowdy pair, always unpredictable and usually involved in fights after drinking sessions at our local watering hole, the L+M Tavern. It was there that we developed our preferred route to an altered consciousness: shots of gin followed by a glass of beer. One day, in such a state, we both decided to quit our jobs and bought motorcycles. For several months we paraded around town like two escaped mental patients. During this time we also began to entertain marijuana, amphetamines, and mescaline as alternatives to alcohol. We were only tolerated because it was a known fact that we were joining the service and would likely be in Vietnam very soon.

The era of peace, love, and self-expression had a captivating hold on us despite the reality being that we were headed to the frontlines of the fight. We were conflicted – torn between war and peace – but committed to our decision. We would have to embrace the war. We were to become *warriors with peace signs*.

As the time of my enlistment drew closer, hardly a day went by that the casualties of war were not brought to my attention. I worried for my brother serving with the Marines in Khe Sanh and began to develop a quiet concern for my own future well-being. Proud and full of youthful enthusiasm, I found myself seeking adventure and wanting to prove who I was. As I readied myself for what was to come, I could not have possibly foreseen that my first great adventure would become a lifelong tragedy.

Shortly before our departure for basic training, Larry and I received word of the wounding of one of our good friends, Bob Hegler. He had left for Vietnam six months earlier and was now back home, in a military hospital in Pennsylvania, after being severely wounded during an attack by the NVA on an outpost he was defending. The images from my hospital visit with him while he was still in critical condition, with injuries to both his arms and his face, left a horrible, lasting impression. The serious nature of his injuries gave me pause for concern. Bob was unable to speak to share what he had experienced; I could only imagine what he had lived through and what he was now feeling.

I now had a first-hand glimpse of how the young men, like myself, who marched off to war did so carrying a false sense of invincibility. The visit brought to mind an anti-war book entitled *Johnny Got His Gun*. The story chronicles the internal dialogue of a young soldier who survived a shelling during World War I only to lose his face and all of his limbs. Left blind, unable to speak or hear, and immobile, he ultimately attempts to communicate with a nurse through the fog of sedation by moving his head. Wanting only to express the horrors and the futility of war that his body epitomized, he soon comes to realize that his caretakers would never let his message leave his bedside.

My brother Fred had returned from Vietnam only about a month or two before I was scheduled to leave. He didn't want to talk much about the war; but, on occasion, if we got wasted, he would open up. The few painful stories that he related of holding fellow soldiers as they were dying and calling out for their mothers were terrifying. Fred gave me the same advice that my father had given me: "Be careful and don't try to be a hero." There really didn't seem to be much more to say to someone as they were departing for war. Bottom line: it was going to be bad. Each man would have to learn for himself. There were no words.

I began the process of preparing for war in the summer of peace that was 1969. The festival at Woodstock was well underway a few two hours north. As I was readying myself to leave for basic training, people were arriving from all over the country to be part of this historic gathering. It was a festival filled with love, peace, and music. Many of my friends were in attendance, bringing all the more to my mind the conflicting nature of the times. *Was it right to be going to war? Was it right that some men chose to avoid service?* When I was young I didn't have a clear understanding of irony, but I seemed to be developing a *very* clear understanding through experience – ironically.

Fort Jackson, South Carolina
1969

As we boarded the flight that would carry us from New York to Fort Jackson, South Carolina, for basic training, I assumed that my buddy Larry and I would accompany each other throughout our time in the service. That was not to be the case. Having quickly developed an intense dislike for the military, Larry managed to get himself run over by a bus in an insane effort to end his military service; his need to return to civilian life and his fiancée were that strong. Despite badly injuring his arm in the incident, the stunt did little more than earn him reassignment to another unit; it did not provide him the desired exit from the Army. At that point we parted company, and I had to struggle through basic infantry training alone. Upon completion of my training, I was assigned the rank of private first class and received my orders to ship out to Vietnam following a 30-day leave.

The mental canvas of a soldier preparing for war portrays the anxiety of anticipation – the fear of unknown challenges to come – painted with the broad, pallid strokes of reality. Getting there was half the battle for prior to ever arriving in the war zone each soldier would struggle with his own emotions. In wars past, getting to the site of combat was a relatively slow process, allowing for a gradual entry into the fray. Conversely, modern day transportation had brought that time down significantly for this war, delivering men to battle much more quickly and efficiently. Now travel to any war zone was possible in one day's time. Men were on the frontlines only some few days after learning their fates, with very little time to process.

Foremost in our minds, though the thought was repeatedly tamped down by our desire to survive, was the potential for death at the hands of our enemy, our fellow man. I had no animus toward people or a country half a world away that I had never seen; yet the image of the Viet Cong and North Vietnamese Army as aggressors was firmly imprinted in my mind during my training as a soldier. Up until that point in my life, any anger that I knew toward my fellow man had been the direct result of some personal interaction and had often been expediently resolved with words or fists. War would not be so simple an endeavor. It was an amassing of men and materials to satisfy a malignant collective anger – a conflict in which an individual's body became not only a weapon but a statistic, a measure of the success of war. War would force us to usher aside our humanity to assume the role of sanctified executioners.

The long-established practice of war, once embraced, inevitably grows in ferocity and scope. Throughout recorded history war has filled the hearts of mothers with the greatest of losses while politicians have clamored to advance its legitimacy. Somehow, man has always failed to avoid the lure of battle as a means of resolving greater disputes despite the inherited assumption that mankind is the reigning species on this planet in terms of intelligence and compassion (or, dare I say, *humanity*).

Vietnam and Cambodia
1970

Once in Vietnam I assumed my position in an infantry line unit with the First Air Cavalry Division; and so began a year of fighting a guerrilla war against the North Vietnamese Army and the Viet Cong in the jungles of Southeast Asia. Watching war unfold from a distance is very different from living it up close. At war you become part of a massive, complex organization whose ultimate goal is to overcome an enemy; at the same time, war is simple and personal, an individual fight for survival. The process of war has changed throughout the centuries, but the final outcome has always been the same: the acquisition of territory and the killing of those who occupy it. As a participant in the invasion of Cambodia in May of 1970, I was party to the capture of the largest weapons cache during the war. It was there that the true cost of war became a personal experience. The sick exhilaration of adrenaline fueled combat; consequently the killing and brutality (on both sides of the conflict) transformed my views of both self and humanity. While pulling guard in the jungle at night, I would often reflect upon where I was and what I was doing. Being allied with danger was such an unfamiliar experience, primitive in its nature. On many occasions, amidst my fear and discomfort, I would challenge my decision to have joined the military and to have tempted fate. My presence here was, to some degree, my own doing; it was a choice that had now become my reality. I could only make the most of this deadly industry – I had to fight to survive.

War is the essence of evil. To see evil work its way through civilized men to the point where they brought harm to one another was dehumanizing. I spent a week in a hospital outside of Saigon after being wounded in Cambodia. There, in my days of convalescence, my waking hours were filled with the sights and sounds of the physical consequences of war. More often than not, those branded by war were young. There were daily processions of wheelchairs carrying those with abbreviated limbs and injuries too unpleasant to recall down the hospital corridors; their wounds were carefully wrapped in white, though many voiced signature red stains. Years of fighting had created well-worn paths in and out of the hospital. While the halls were filled with the residue of trauma and last words, both sides seemed willing to embrace these casualties of conflict in their quest for domination. Human life was the exchange, the freely-spent currency of war. The precious nature of a solitary life is immeasurable, its loss saddening; the combined loss of the hundreds of thousands of lives that this war had claimed seemed the work of demons. I was one of the fortunate. Discharged from the hospital, I spent the remainder of my time in Vietnam in a non-combat capacity. I counted my blessings, thankful for each day that reluctantly passed while I awaited my time to return home from war. Time takes on a different tempo at war; it almost seemed compressed, making some days feel like a lifetime. I waited the way a survivor does: grateful, apprehensive, and constantly wondering why my life was spared when so many others met a different fate.

Staten Island, New York
Late 1960's – Early 1970's

Addiction is a peculiar thing. As much a part of mankind's evolution as anything else, addiction has paraded throughout recorded history as a common bond between the primitive and the refined. Creating a compound reversal of perceived rewards, it has been (and continues to be) an aberrant acquaintance offering everything while delivering nothing.

As children we had witnessed so many of the evils of alcohol consumption in the faces of those who sat around our kitchen table seeking our father's counsel. One would have thought that such first-hand exposure would have ensured that none us would ever fall prey to the demon ourselves. Unfortunately, that was not the case for any of us, including my sister, Annie. Like her namesake (my mother's aunt) she was very generous, always ready to bring a smile or to lend a hand whenever needed. She was smart, good-looking, and had a wonderful sense of humor...but the curse of alcohol had befallen her nonetheless.

It slowly worked its way into her life, infiltrating early on in high school, well before she had reached the legal drinking age of 18. Sneaking a few beers here and a mixed drink there with her friends, Annie soon realized that alcohol brought her the same warmth and freedom from inhibitions that had lured so many before her into the waiting, loving arms of addiction. She became more heavily invested in her addiction during the time that I was in the service. Before venturing out to the clubs on Friday nights, she would gather her friends around our kitchen table to drink (after my father had gone to an AA meeting with his most recent charge). Annie perceived her drinking as merely social, all in good fun; but, although these social events may have been innocent in nature, they were ritualistic enough to allow the early seeds of alcoholism to be planted.

A compounding problem for Annie was the type of men she gravitated toward; they were all, in a word, wanting. Most of these men were heavy drinkers and that inevitably paved the way for stormy relationships. Each new acquaintance was seemingly worse than the last, until she met Buddy Geisler. A non-smoker, *light* drinker, and a hard worker, Buddy was a decorated Green Beret who had recently returned from Vietnam at the time of their meeting. He was a solid candidate for a stable relationship. Annie had finally met someone who could offer her a better life and help to delay the grip of the curse. Some short time later, Annie and Buddy were engaged to be married. All preparations were underway: they found a house, made a down payment, and prepared for their future together.

I was just back to the United States from Vietnam, serving the last six months of my enlistment in Fort Benning, Georgia, when I received a message to call home. The news was not good: the future Annie had been planning with Buddy would never come to be. He had been killed when the utility truck he was riding in hit a telephone pole. It was a great shock, and everyone was distraught. I got an emergency leave to return to New York. I'd never seen my sister like this; she was a mess. It hurt to see her engulfed in grief – her fiancée, her future, and her life all seemingly lost. Fate had taken everything from her in an instant. Our words provided no comfort; they seemed to fall short of the consolation she so badly needed. We could only stand beside her in her time of grief. Time would be necessary for healing.

Annie seemed lost in a spiritual and physical vacuum. There was a space in time that was gone and could never be duplicated. She was drowning in emptiness, and her overwhelming sorrow provided fertile soil for the seeds of alcoholism (planted long ago) to take root. Having laid her love to rest, the anesthetic for one of life's greatest traumas was found in a bottle. Cloaked in the mourning clothes of a friend, shadowed by a dark veil that masked its true intentions, and with gentle persuasions, the curse drew her closer. Alcohol delivered the comfort and consolation our words had been unable to provide.

***

Who amongst us has not, at times, desired to be in another place, both mentally and physically? To find a means of relief, a separation from what ails us? At the core of addiction lies the desire to feel good, peaceful, and content – such an uncomplicated and natural desire. Sought after by each of us, it is a desire that is quite easy to understand. The question is how we each seek to achieve that feeling and the lengths to which we will go to maintain it. If we will go so far as to sacrifice self-control in doing so, we may find ourselves standing at the gateway to addiction.

The original sin of the addicted is their first bite of that forbidden fruit of escape. The temptation is enticing, but we cannot (legitimately) consciously divorce ourselves from reality by ingesting something. To do so results in a disproportionate amount of pain for the amount of peace we might achieve. The end result will only be a broken helix of discontent as the pieces of our life slowly become unraveled.

Fort Benning, Georgia
1971

By every measure, the war that I fought in had been complicated. Our countrymen and leaders alike were divided over the legitimacy of the conflict. Unable to gain a total victory or an honorable disengagement, our men were left to endure the fighting on the frontlines of this stalemate until U.S. troops eventually withdrew in 1973. The capture of Saigon in April 1975 marked the end of the war, at which time Vietnam was declared a communist country.

This war had been fought one year at a time. Those who were lucky returned after serving 365 days. An unlucky 58,267 perished before their year of service had ended. I was one of the lucky ones. I returned home happy to be alive, but I found that the war had left me emotionally bankrupt; the capital of sensitivity had become a callused currency. Wanting to appear normal, I donned the mask of the combat veteran. As old as the wars of man, it was a mask that had graced the countenances of returning warriors throughout recorded time; an expression conjured by the mind to soften the hardened look of those who bore the brunt of battle, sparing loved ones the stories of pain and death that war had etched into their faces. My mask, sometimes transparent to those who knew me well, was opaque to the casual acquaintance and impenetrable to the stranger. I only removed it to show my true face in the presence of those who wore masks themselves.

There was a rage that dwelled inside of me. That rage was temporarily subdued by repatriation as there were healing effects to a normal and peaceful environment. Peace seemed to be the balm necessary to soothe the scars of war – but those scars were deep, and I soon learned the balm of peace could not work forever. Occasionally my scars would reopen, spilling trauma and bad memories into my dreams and conscious mind. Each time this happened, the darkness of the past would reawaken with a vengeance. So began a considerably troubled period of my life.

Staten Island, New York
Early 1970's

The psychological terms and definitions so often used to describe those returning from war had become my reality. *PTSD, paranoia, startle response, hyper vigilance, intrusive thoughts, nightmares,* and *anger* – all of these psychological phenomena were bandied about by the Veterans Administration psychologists. They did their best to help but fell short of solving my issues with war. Their reliance on medications did nothing more than send me off in search of alternative ways to deal with my new, troubled self. My brother and most of my close friends, having all seen war up close and personally, were also part of this masked generation of Americans seeking relief from who we had become. The city streets were a pharmaceutical wonderland for those of us seeking to alter our consciousness...and we all grew increasingly dependent on the escape. If we were down, we could be brought up. If we were too tense, we could be brought down. If we felt normal, a psychotropic would bring the world alive in a way previously unimagined. I never consciously used drugs to ease the pain of combat, but they certainly seemed to help bridge the distance between me and society.

In the first few years after my homecoming, my friends and I would party with a vengeance. Wild celebrations were not uncommon for our age group, but our all-consuming (too-near-death) experiences occurred far too frequently. Drugs became a daily indulgence, and we tended to test the limits to which we could become stoned. Without realizing it, the yoke of alcohol had gradually been lifted from my neck only to be replaced by a seemingly less burdensome but, nevertheless, destructive bondage.

No one stopped to consider the consequences or the appropriateness of what we were doing. We didn't think in terms of right or wrong, we just instinctively sought the break from reality. No one blamed the war outright for our debauchery; most times we didn't even talk about the war at all. Our indulgence in drugs and mayhem – and our mounting insanity – had simply become our life. This behavior continued for several years until I had a startling insight after several troubling drug-related incidents.

On one occasion I had a really bad toothache. I had tried, to no avail, to self-medicate the pain with a variety of means. Eventually, I managed to get an appointment with a dentist late on a Friday afternoon. I convinced the dental assistant that I needed nitrous oxide for the procedure; it was just another means of achieving that altered state of consciousness I had come to enjoy. Already stoned when I arrived, the gas put me over the edge of reality as soon as it started to pump. Quick as you could say "Jumping Jack Flash" I was really out of it. Now, I was quite familiar with hallucinogens (and a host of other drugs), but what I was experiencing was something completely new: I was paralyzed, hallucinating, and paranoid all at the same time. It was a frightening experience. Lying there, unable to speak or move, I became concerned that they had forgotten I was even in the chair. After all, it was Friday afternoon, and I was an unscheduled patient; I was convinced that they had all gone home. *Holy shit! I'm going to be in here for the weekend.* I hoped that they would at least leave the lights on. No one knew that I had gone to the dentist, so there would be no search party looking for me. It's hard to explain the degree of fright I was experiencing. My body had become something distinctively separate from my mind, which was racing wildly. Time had ceased to exist, and I dwelled in a perpetual moment of apprehension. I could not tell how long I had been there already, but I was sure that I would be trapped there for a long time. Suddenly, I saw the dentist's masked face in front of me. He seemed to be moving very quickly while asking in an excited tone if I was all right. At that point he would've been better off having asked me to blink once for 'yes' and twice for 'no.' After he administered some straight oxygen, I gradually started coming to my senses. I told him I was okay (which really wasn't true, but it seemed like the right thing to say at the time). At least I didn't jump from the chair screaming like a maniac. Needless to say, the dentist performed the procedure simply using Novocain. I learned later that the assistant had failed to give me enough oxygen along with the gas; that mistake could have done (and perhaps did) some real damage to my brain.

On another occasion I had gone to a doctor at the Veterans Administration for a skin condition I felt was related to my exposure to Agent Orange. After some preliminary tests, he told me in no uncertain terms, "You better stop whatever you are doing. It's catching up to you." No part of my body seemed to be working correctly. My physical condition was completely deteriorating, and my thinking was truly screwed up; I found myself always wanting to be somewhere other than where I was. It was truly ironic that throughout my childhood I had witnessed the effects of addiction from the outside in, and now I was witnessing it from the inside out. The world I knew was slowly closing in around me. I found myself sick in body, mind, and spirit, aching in a life that I had cherished and fought so hard to preserve while in Vietnam. I was surrounded by family and friends; yet lonelier I could not have been. I wanted – I needed – to reestablish a simple gratitude for living, to once again appreciate the precious nature of life and the joy of being a conscious living thing.

Call it a revelation, seeing the light, or just being sick of grinding through each day while hoping for a better life; I finally understood very clearly that unless I stopped the drugs, they would kill me – period. This was now the choice before me: quit or die. The importance of that choice was heightened by the experience of an aneurysm in my left arm, the result of a prolonged period of excessive use of amphetamines. It could've killed me – a refrain that had become all too familiar. Despite all of the negative things I'd seen in my life, I chose to live.

***

After my Aunt Mary and Uncle Jim (Uncle Wow-Wow) moved on, we took a short hiatus from renting out the apartment on the second floor (to family or anyone else for that matter). It didn't take too long, though, before the empty apartment called out for a tenant. My parents had become familiar with a couple named Clara and Ronald Gleason, who happened to be looking for a place to live; and so, along with their teenage daughter, Denise, they soon became our newest tenants. My parents had met the couple at a group they attended each week where they would read and discuss the work of Emmett Fox (a writer, medium, and healer/prognosticator who was popular among metaphysicians in the early 1900's). The group was hosted at the home of a woman in her later years named Harriett Inman, a long-standing follower of Fox. Part of their weekly gatherings would include a period where Clara would enter a trance-like state and channel spirits from the other side.

My father was never overtly religious, but he desperately sought and quietly pursued a deeper understanding of life through reading. His spiritual library was extensive, covering everything from the Bible, the Vedas, and the Torah to mysticism of every sort. He felt there was a common link between all beliefs in their worship of God, and he sought to expose himself to as many views of God as he possibly could. Even though he was raised Catholic, he had engaged in the exploration of the metaphysical community for some years in search of knowledge that would bring a greater connection to God and Creation. Ever the skeptic, he found Clara to be (what he called) "the real thing." The insights, inspiration, knowledge, and comfort he found in her words brought an enrichment of his spiritual nature.

Clara was an interesting woman. She was pleasant, quick to laughter, and generous. In every sense of the word – except for her eyes and the fact that she communicated with the dead – she seemed "normal" to me. I had a habit of looking directly into people's eyes while talking to them, but with Clara I always found myself feeling uncomfortable when our eyes connected. Her eyes bore an unusual strength, a piercing intensity, which would often cause me to casually divert my gaze to break the connection. Her stare was so penetrating that I felt as though she was able to look inside me, capable of seeing things that others could not. At first it made me a little uneasy, but as I got to know her better I learned her all-seeing eyes were of no consequence.

Clara always downplayed her psychic abilities; she would not talk about them at length. I did find out some interesting things about her gift in our brief conversations, though. As far back as she could remember, she had a mysterious insight into people. Given that her abilities developed during her childhood, she assumed everyone else shared in what she was experiencing. She could see a person's aura; over time she better understood the changing colors and intensities of the energy surrounding a person's body, and could, thus, read a great deal about them. When in grade school, she became aware that she could always tell when someone was lying. She would hear one of her friends or classmates say something that was not true and would be shocked to see the lie accepted. Unsure as to why this would happen and believing that everyone else saw the world as she did, she reasoned that it must be a game people played. As she grew older, however, it became apparent that her world of perception was far different from that of those with whom she interacted. She kept what she knew to herself, fearing ridicule or alienation, especially in her teenage years. Keeping her insights to herself was difficult; it became even harder to do as her perception began to include seeing the spirits of the deceased. With no one to explain or help guide her with what she was experiencing, her life became troubled. Eventually, the struggle to keep her gift silenced led her into the comforting arms of alcohol. Unable to distance herself from who she was, she suffered under the influence for many years until she ultimately found relief through the fellowship of AA.

Once her life stabilized, Clara began to share her ability with the public. Before long she had a large following of people who wanted to reconnect with their loved ones reaching out to her. People from all over the country would seek out her services; most, if not all, were shocked by her ability to share a dialogue with their dearly-departed. She was sought out by people wanting to say a last goodbye, clear up a misunderstanding from the past, say things that they had always wanted to say, or just share a simple "I love you." As rewarding as it was to provide this service, her work took a toll on her. She would say that it was very draining, both physically and emotionally, to carry out these psychic readings (as she would call them).

Clara typically performed her readings at the home of Harriett Inman, the very place where my parents had first become acquainted with her at their Fox discussion meetings. Located in an upscale neighborhood, it was a stately house set alongside a lake on a quiet, tree-lined street. Harriett would assist Clara in her sessions in a small, antique-filled, candlelit room on the second floor.

My father once had an individual session with Clara; not knowing what he might encounter from his past, he was anxious. Clara began each session with a little prayer. She would then sit quietly with her eyes closed before falling into a state of shallow breathing. She would suddenly erupt with a voice (not her own) announcing a dramatic "welcome" to those present. Without a great deal of fanfare, she would then identify the spirits who were present and interested in the company around her. Clara told my father there were many spirits there who sought to greet him: his parents, friends from World War II, and a mysterious man wearing a long, dark coat. The session was going well, with questions going back and forth, but then the mysterious man was insistent on speaking. He said only one thing: "I forgive you." As Clara began to give a better description of this mysterious figure, my father's demeanor began to change. He suddenly jumped up, bolted from the room, and ran right out of the house. He never gave any indication as to who this dark figure might have been, or what he was being forgiven for; the feeling was that it was probably better we didn't know. So ended my father's first contact with the spirit world; we talked no further about the encounter.

I also had my own unusual experience in a session with Clara. Interested in seeking out the intangible aspects of life, I asked her for a personal reading; she welcomed the request. I remember the night very clearly. It was in the fall; I made my way down the tree-lined street to Harriett Inman's house in the darkness. As I shuffled through the leaves that blanketed the sidewalk, I slowed my pace to a contemplative stroll. Having seen the impact a reading had on my father (who was not upset by many things), I felt unusually anxious. I didn't know quite what to expect from the upcoming encounter. I wondered who might be there waiting to communicate with me. I wanted to know more; yet I was fearful of what I did not know. At the last moment, as I drew close to the house, I had a sudden case of metaphysical apprehension. I wondered if perhaps I should rethink my exploration of the unknown. *What was it that I was looking for that I didn't already know? Would this experience be cathartic or just a whimsical exercise? Who might be there waiting for a chance to speak with me? Would I want to hear what they had to say?*

I had only recently returned from my year in Vietnam; and so I imagined those who had perished beside me there would likely seek to make their presence known. A quick thought of those lost and the circumstances of their sudden deaths caused me both mental and physical pain. This wasn't the first time such thoughts conjured up pain within me. I had started to experience the haunting presence of those who died alongside me in combat while I was recovering in the hospital in Vietnam from the injuries I'd suffered in Cambodia. Their faces, their voices, and their final expressions were all part of the legacy I inherited from war. Visiting whether I was awake or asleep, they came not to torment but to somehow seek comfort. They would congregate around those who held their memory, those who shared in their lives and their pain but not in their deaths. *Could I have been the final face they saw? Did I hear their final words? Did I offer them some parting prayer?* Their lifelong companionship was the price I paid for having known them at war. *Was it wrong to try to resurrect them? Would it not now be better to simply leave them at peace?*

    As I climbed the steps to ring the doorbell, I continued to wonder toward what end I was seeking out those who no longer lived. Harriett greeted me at the door and led me to the living room where Clara awaited. We sat for a time making small talk before retiring to the small, candlelit room where Clara did her readings. The antiquated wooden stairs seemed to speak volumes with each step that drew upon them for support as we ascended to the second floor. We three sat in a circle, facing each other. I settled back in the comfortable old armchair while Harriett explained what would follow. The flickering of the candles created an eerie yet peaceful atmosphere of animated shadows. The smell of incense entertained my senses. Clara said a simple prayer before slipping into a trance-like state. In the quiet of that moment, I felt as though I had entered into the vestiges of some secret society where uncommon knowledge was shared; my interest was piqued all the more. I thought of the mysterious society of Masons (amongst whom were the founding fathers of our country) known for their rituals and secret meetings. My thoughts were quickly interrupted when Clara suddenly began to speak in a peculiar voice, with a distinct cadence. "Welcome," she said loudly; she spoke with a dialect that I could not quite place. The volume of the greeting was in sharp contrast to the silence that had just preceded it. "We wish you all peace and love in this time and place. It is good to be with you. There are many gathering here, sending much love your way. They are pleased with your progress in this lifetime, knowing that you have achieved many goals that you had set to accomplish in your time on this earth. We see the sadness that surrounds you from your time at war."

Clara had my undivided attention as she continued to speak in the stranger's voice: "It was a time for you of great fear and regret. It has caused a scarring of your being and a loss of confidence in life, but it is done. You will move on and experience happiness in this life. There are those here who fought with you at that time. One soul here seeks to tell you that there was nothing you could do. His name is Andy. Do you know who this is?" Shocked, I confirmed that I knew exactly who Andy was: he had fought beside me before being captured and later killed during a mission while we were in Cambodia. "He continues to say there was nothing you could do; it was his fate. He says emphatically that you don't need to carry the guilt of his capture." Shaken by the revelation, I felt compelled to speak and ask questions, but I was off-balance. Not knowing what to say or do, I simply sat in an awkward silence as Clara continued: "He speaks of the dark, rainy hillside in Cambodia where you fought a losing battle with the NVA, and of his unfortunate capture and execution by his captors." I wondered how it was possible that these intimate, painful things I had experienced were being revealed before me. There was no way anyone could know of these things, much less my thoughts regarding my involvement. I felt naked – stripped of all concealment, completely exposed – as if my thoughts were projected, uncensored, upon a screen for all to see. I was experiencing a strange psychic intrusion; yet I had a sense of comfortable, deep relief at the same time. *Who is it other than myself who can open such long-closed doors deep within me? Is my mind so easily accessed? Are there really no secrets then in life?*

I was caught up in a whirlwind of emotion, fascinated by the realization that the barriers which seemingly exist between life and death could actually be overcome. I anxiously forced myself to listen in pursuit of answers as Clara spoke: "There are others here who seek to speak with you. An Army lieutenant who fought with you has come forward. Lieutenant Morgan. Do you know him?" I said that I did. "He says that he appreciates having served with you and that you should not be troubled by the incident that took his life. He knows that you endlessly relive those heart-wrenching events, and he is aware of the last vision you have of him lying dead on the jungle floor. He wants you to know he is at peace. He hopes that you can let those sad images go and be happy in this life. Do you understand?" I understood.

Lieutenant Morgan was killed during the Cambodian invasion. For the short time that he had been our platoon leader in the Army's First Air Cavalry Division, I had served as his radioman, and we had become close. He was a good leader; he was conscientious, cheerful, dedicated, and always concerned for his men. The circumstances of his death were all the more tragic because it was the result of a fatal accident; it was a random, ill-fated consequence of the deadly tools of war, suffered outside of battle. Death at the hands of the enemy is to be expected at war; however, death as a result of an accident was perceived as a much worse fate. We had been in Cambodia for only a short period of time, maybe two weeks. We were occupying a recently-captured North Vietnamese weapons depot, helping to remove the captured material and running patrols through the surrounding countryside in search of the enemy. Early in the morning of May 13, 1970, as the sun was just beginning to work its way through the thick jungle surrounding the cache site, I sat with the lieutenant. As the morning mist began to fade, we discussed what patrols we would be running that day. He was readying himself to move outside our perimeter with two sergeants (nicknamed Batman and Frenchy) to check on their progress in setting up automatic ambushes in defense of our position. These safeguards involved the use of an explosive device called the claymore mine that would self-detonate once a tripwire was sprung; it was a powerful weapon and deadly at close range. As radioman it was customary for me to be with the lieutenant, with the radio, wherever he went. Accordingly, when Lieutenant Morgan rose to leave, I grabbed my radio and began to do the same; but he told me it wouldn't be necessary to accompany him as they were not going far outside the perimeter. His final words to me would be "Stay here and make yourself some coffee. We will be back shortly." And with that, he quickly disappeared into the brush with the two sergeants.

Following his directive, I took the opportunity to prepare some coffee and began to heat some water in my canteen cup. No more than five minutes after the lieutenant and sergeants had left my side, a huge explosion tore through the quiet morning air. Immediately following the explosion, I heard their desperate screams for help; I can still hear the anguished voices of our brothers calling out to us. When we reached their location, we were shocked by what we saw; I continue to see their devastating injuries. Batman was still conscious but had lost his legs. His clothes were torn from his body as the medics worked feverishly to stem his bleeding and reassure him that he would be okay. Frenchy lay motionless with numerous wounds covering his body; he seemed barely alive. Lieutenant Morgan's face was an ashen color; his body was surrounded by shredded vegetation from the blast, and he had but one wound on his right temple – a wound that had taken his life. I had been in the combat zone for five months, and I had seen my share of guerrilla warfare with its attendant demoralization – the result of the extremes endured by body and mind in the face of catastrophic situations – but this was the experience and the image that would always prove most painful to recall.

Having sufficiently reacquainted myself with the war during this reading with Clara, I was somewhat relieved when she went on to talk about things that were less painful; admittedly, I was only half listening at that point as I was still processing my initial visitors. Clara slowly returned to us as the session ended. When she asked what I thought of the reading, all I could manage as a response was "It was good." Despite the spiraling chain of questions in my mind, I found it difficult to verbalize them to pursue answers. Uncertain if I wanted to know any more information or what else might be uncovered, I declined any further exchange. I thanked Clara for her insights as we rose and made our way from the room. I could now understand how my father (with his wild life) could have been freaked out by God knows what was revealed to him during his reading. I bid Clara and Harriett a good night and retreated to the safety of the neighborhood bar, where I proceeded to get wasted with my friends. As I shared the stories of my recent encounter with the afterworld, my friends directed the bartender to get me another beer and, in their best sarcastic voices, suggested a few more drinks be served for my unseen friends.

Having Clara live in our house was truly (as we said in those days) "a trip." She would often share with us the things that we were unaware of – those things that she alone would see – that were occurring in the house. She said that there were always unusual things happening in this old home; because the house was over 200 years old, a lot of old energy had accumulated over time and some spirits still dwelled there. It was great to hear her talk about such things; my imagination always conjured up images to illustrate the sightings she would describe. Soon after she moved into the apartment, she told us that the three sisters – Mini, Nora, and my grandmother, Hannah – were still around and still arguing amongst themselves. She joked that they were not helping with the rent. Moving about from room to room, Clara would often encounter older spirits with whom she would converse. Her sightings were frequent and would occur in both the light of day and the darkness of night. Clara always spoke of such things in a very down-to-earth, matter-of-fact way, never excited or shocked by what was happening. These were the things she saw; and, whether anyone else believed it or not, this was her life. Lights would often flicker on and off around her. One day, while she was cleaning, the broom she was sweeping with remained standing upright in the middle of the room after it had left her hands. Her understanding of such things was that, knowing her sensitivity to their presence, the spirits were seeking to make contact with her in order to communicate with their loved ones.

Based upon the number of charlatans who took advantage of people in times of grief, there were many people who were skeptical of Clara's abilities, but I found her to be both credible and altruistic. I had seen her help many people while she lived with us; people were always coming and going. She brought them a special comfort, freed them from guilt, and united them with loved ones so that they could achieve a rare form of closure. She may have had a difficult time accepting her unique gift at first, but she had certainly gone on to make the most of it.

Eastern Pennsylvania
Summer 1959

There were very few things that bothered my mother; if they did, you would never have known it. There was one thing, however, that clearly haunted her through the years. It was a near-fatal incident that occurred in the mountains of eastern Pennsylvania in 1959, while we were on our first real vacation. The incident still resides in my collection of permanent, vivid nightmares. We had rented a small, rustic cabin hidden away in a dense grove of pine trees in a little town called Rowlands on the Lackawaxen River. My father would come up on the weekends, while my mother, with four children ages 6 through 11, remained during the week. There were no phones and no television, only a small radio that played more static than music; but we were content to be out of the city, enjoying the newness, the quiet, and beauty of it all. It seemed that the world was a more civilized place in those days; the joys of childhood were best expressed. Without electronic gizmos for entertainment, we played together with board games and BB guns. Our days were spent outdoors, filled with explorations and regular trips to a nearby mountain stream. It was a good time for us.

One weekday morning we all made our way down to the Lackawaxen River (a wide river that flowed into the vast Delaware River some few miles downstream). It was a gorgeous day, sunny with a deep blue sky. The river was not very deep where we chose to picnic; it was maybe waist high at its deepest. My mother had purposely chosen this location because she could not swim and, thus, always had a fear of the water. We enjoyed our lunch (which was always peanut butter and jelly, or bologna sandwiches) and Kool-Aid before playing along the shallow banks of the rocky river throughout the afternoon, looking for frogs and searching the sky for a glimpse of an eagle or a hawk. After enough hours in the sun, we decided it was time to head back to the cabin. My brother Fred and I suggested that we just walk across the river; at that point it was only about 300 feet across. It would be a much shorter route than having to return to the small bridge (a few hundred yards away) that we had crossed to get to our picnic area. So, with our towels and gear in tow, the five of us began the slow crossing of the river. Fred led the way, followed closely by me and Annie. My mother reluctantly trailed behind us, helping my younger brother, Jimmy. What was unknown to us at the time was that the river was fed upstream by a hydroelectric dam that generated electricity locally. When the dam was producing electricity, huge amounts of water flooded into the river, causing the water level to quickly rise several feet and, thereby, create a powerful downstream current.

It all happened in an instant. It started with the appearance of floating debris, vegetation, and wood; then the water turned an ominous, murky brown. Suddenly, the water rose higher, and the current grew stronger. By the time we realized what was happening, we were already in the grasp of the rising water. Each of us scrambled to find a way back to the shore. Fred was the furthest out but managed to fight his way back to where the rest of us were; we were all struggling to keep our heads above water. My mother, who was closest to the shore, frantically fought her way out of the water with Jimmy before returning to help Annie, who was yelling and flailing nearby. I had managed to grab hold of the top of a large, protruding rock; holding as tight as I could (for dear life), my body was horizontal from the force of the water. I watched as my mother, amidst her greatest fear, grabbed Annie's arm and pulled her to safety. Fred managed to get to my location to do the same for me. Once out of harm's way – and exhausted – we all collapsed on the shore as the turbulent river sped by with fury.

We all sat in shock at what had happened in the course of just some few minutes. Had we been only a little bit further out into that river, it would've been a tragic day. My mother was terrified by the incident, as were we all. We slowly gathered our things (those that hadn't washed downstream) and began to back away from the shoreline, distancing ourselves from the ominous threat. We had shared a trauma that none of us would ever forget – it was a swirling trauma that would lodge itself deeply in our collective psyche. We now saw the river as potentially deadly and never swam in it again. Eventually, after some less fortunate people drowned, signs were posted along the banks of the river to alert swimmers of the dangerous surges in water level that could unexpectedly occur.

Great Kills, Staten Island
Early 1960's

Years later there was another water-related incident that caused my mother great upset. This time it involved me and two friends on the waters that surrounded Staten Island. At the age of 16, I set out for a day of fun, sun, and beer with two of my friends, Ray and Kenny. Ray happened to own a small boat but, having had trouble with the boat's engine, we spent most of the day drinking on the dock while the engine was serviced by a mechanic in the marina. The weather was nice and warm for an early June weekend, and so we stripped down to our bathing suits to enjoy the sun. Later that afternoon, once the engine had been repaired, we set out for a ride on the water. We were all drunk at that point and reveled in some crazy maneuvers on our way out of Great Kills Harbor. Ray was a genuine madman; he took great joy in scaring the hell out of us, running at full speed toward the large, steel buoys that served as channel markers only to swerve at the last second to avoid them. It was very dangerous.

The sun was low in the sky as we moved further away from the shore. Having cleared the harbor, we headed straight out toward the shipping lanes that connected the ocean to New York City. Suddenly, several miles out, our joyous romp across the waves came to a sudden end when we hit a large submerged piece of wood that ripped the propeller right off the engine. The force of the impact was so great that I thought we might sink. The tiny boat shuddered, the engine stopped, and we were instantly "dead in the water." Miles offshore, the sun about to set, we all gave a collective sigh of relief that we were at least still afloat. We even laughed for a moment about how lucky we had been. Then the harsh reality of the situation set in: we had no radio to call for help, no oars or paddles to try to move the boat, no life jackets, no clothes beyond the bathing suits we were wearing, and no real food or drink. We were in sight of land but unable to alert anyone to where we were.

Prone to seasickness, the bobbing and rolling of the tiny boat brought my beer-filled belly to a heightened state of nausea. In between my bouts of puking, we discussed our options. With darkness setting in, the sizable distance to land, the fact that we had no life jackets, and the realization that we didn't even know which way the tide was moving, the idea of trying to swim to shore was far too dangerous. We were stranded. We hoped that, by chance, a boat would come close enough to our location so we could signal to them that we were in distress...but that didn't happen. And then darkness fell. Despite how sunny and warm the day had been, it was June; and the nights still got cool this time of year. As we were all sunburned from our day of drinking on the dock, we felt that coolness even more as the night slowly wore on. I could literally feel the heat radiating from my body as I shivered and tried to contain the sound of my chattering teeth. We were all freezing and beginning to experience hypothermia.

Floating around in the darkness through the night, while the waves crashed in an offbeat rhythm against the side of the boat, was a strange feeling. Puking every so often was the only thing that broke the monotony of the rolling boat. The shoreline and the lights of the city all seemed so close, yet were so far away. We all stared at that shoreline, wishing we were there. We hoped that someone would discover our clothing and empty beer cans on the dock and perhaps realize that we had not returned. It occurred to me that our families were going to be freaked out when they discovered we were missing. We did have a watch, but that only seemed to accentuate the torturously slow passing of time. By 1:00 a.m. we felt sure that our families must have been trying to determine our whereabouts. Surely they would have contacted the Coast Guard to begin a search.

As we continued to stare at the shoreline, we realized that we were moving further away from land; that meant we were moving closer to the shipping lanes that ran through the harbor. At first we thought it might help to be in a highly-trafficked area, but we soon realized it would also be very dangerous. The huge cargo ships coming in and out of the New York City harbor could roll right over us without ever even knowing they had hit something. As if the idea of getting hit by a cargo ship wasn't bad enough, my thoughts focused on their massive propellers that chopped away at the water – and anything else – in their paths. I was petrified. Our boat was only about 14-feet long, and the bow and stern lights did little to display our position in the darkness.

Between the shivering cold and the fear of what might hit us, none of us were able to sleep. Ray had curled up in the back of the boat, I was in the middle seat, and Kenny was up front. We strained our eyes throughout the night, hoping to see a boat close enough to our location that they might be able to hear us if we yelled. We shared the only sustenance we had aboard; it seemed fittingly ironic that happened to be half a roll of Lifesavers. We had nothing to drink, and I found myself terribly thirsty from all the excitement. We spoke very little. We endured a most unpleasant evening, worrying as much for ourselves as for our parents as we knew they would be frantically trying to locate us throughout the night. I knew that my parents would have to be deeply concerned; my failure to return home had certainly suggested something was seriously wrong.

We were woefully unprepared for such a situation, and it would be a lesson that would stay with me for the rest of my life. In the distance to our west was Newark airport in New Jersey. Planes circled all night in their landing sequence; it was unsettling to know that there were so many people (millions, in fact) who were so close but unaware of our plight, unable to help. Their lives continued comfortably despite our predicament. Separated from everything brought to mind how small we were in the grand scheme of things – so small beneath the star-lit sky.

"Hey, what the hell is that? I think I see a UFO." Kenny's abrupt declaration brought our focus to a series of lights moving in a peculiar way over the skies of New York City. By now we were all suffering from the effects of exposure, and so it didn't take much convincing that we were witnessing something of a mirage. Our bizarre sighting, in fact, did not exist; it had merely been an intense group hallucination, and it failed to hold our attention for very long before we each returned to the stupor we had all fallen into as the night had worn on.

As the hours slowly passed, I became increasingly conscious of the amount of heat leaving my body; the shivering seemed to increase to a point where I felt like I was dancing. It is surprising how quickly the body can succumb to the effects of lower temperatures. I tried desperately to retain some heat by wrapping my arms around my legs as I waited for morning to bring some relief. Finally, we all caught a glimpse of the impending sunrise. It was a welcomed sight – a real sight – that offered the first bit of encouragement since we were first stranded. It was Sunday morning, and the light of day gradually crept upon us. The increasing warmth of the sun began to ease the discomfort of the cold night. We expected that we would soon see the Coast Guard as they would certainly have been searching for us. Or perhaps a passing fishing boat would spot us and bring us to safety; after all, we were in an area that was usually well-traveled by both commercial fishermen and those recreational fishermen out for a day on the water from the many local marinas. Our expectations thwarted, we remained adrift for hours after that welcomed sunrise.

As the sun rose higher, it burned stronger in the sky, paining our already-sunburned bodies. We had moved from one extreme to another – from freezing to burning – and it was hard to tell which one was worse. Thirst had now become our major focus; we were all dehydrated (drinking so much beer on the dock the day before had only compounded the situation). I had never been so thirsty in my life. The poem "The Rime of the Ancient Mariner" came to mind, specifically the passage "Water, water everywhere. Nor any drop to drink." That line was certainly written by someone who had experienced a situation like the one at hand. The absence of simply having something to drink was a powerful deprivation, and it was all I could think about at that moment.

Finally, we spotted a boat. It was a good distance from us, but we still waved our arms, yelling wildly to try to get their attention. They did see us, but they only waved back. We couldn't be sure if they had realized our situation; if they had, we assumed they had just been willing to let us wait for some other passerby to deal with. The unspoken rule of boating is that if you see someone in distress, you either have to tow them to shore yourself or get help for them. Being that it was Sunday morning, we felt these folks were probably out for recreation, and so the thought of spending hours getting us back to shore was not appealing. Believe it or not, this happened several times throughout the morning – waves but no help – until around eleven o'clock when a cabin cruiser drew near, circling our tiny boat to ask what the problem was. *At last!* The boater said he would tow us back to the marina from whence we had begun our journey. He radioed the Coast Guard and was informed they had been out searching for us. Our parents were already at the marina, awaiting our arrival. *Oh shit*, I thought. As happy as I was to be getting towed in, I knew that what awaited me at the dock would not be good. Getting drunk, boating ill-prepared and becoming stranded, and worrying my parents sick was surely a recipe for catching hell from my father.

The captain of the cabin cruiser applied a little too much gas to the throttle as he began to tow us; the sudden surge threw us all to the floor and nearly swamped our boat. Looking back, he yelled his apologies before proceeding toward the marina. The ride seemed to take forever, and the diesel fumes from the cabin cruiser's engine were making us all sick. As we sat in tow, I reflected on our experience at sea. Being stranded and unable to change the outcome of the situation manifested a feeling of helplessness I had never experienced before. It gave me a whole new respect for – and fear of – the ocean. It also taught me the necessity of being as prepared as possible whenever venturing out into nature. Exposure can be deadly, and it evidently comes on quickly, with devastating effects; enduring only one night had beaten us up pretty badly. It was an experience that would stay with me long after we returned to shore.

As we neared the harbor and the marina came into sight, I could see our fathers awaiting us at the dock alongside a Coast Guard ship. They seemed to yell out in unison: "Are you guys all right?" Always stern, my father was surprisingly calm as he offered me a hand to get out of the boat. The same was true of Kenny's father, another steadfast product of World War II. They had both certainly considered the possibility of our demise during the search; we had, regrettably, forced them to live a parent's worst nightmare. Ray's family was conspicuous by their absence; such was his family life that we wondered if they had even realized he was missing.

We yelled our thanks to our rescuer as the cabin cruiser returned to sea. My mouth was so dry that I found it difficult to even speak; I had to get something to drink. My father gave me some change, and I made my way to a nearby coke machine where I proceeded to down two bottles of soda; I then promptly began puking all over the dock. After I had recovered from my shameless display, my father simply said, "Call your mother. You have her worried sick." I made my way to the payphone at the end of the dock to call home and ease her concerns. As I had assumed, once they had realized that we were somewhere out on the water, my parents worried throughout the night. Discovering our clothes and empty beer cans on the dock had only served to magnify their fears.

I was a mess. I was sunburned and dehydrated, suffering from exposure and seasickness, and nauseas from the diesel fumes produced by our towboat. I told Kenny and Ray I would see them later as I followed my father to our car in the parking lot. The ride home was a quiet one. I gave an honest accounting of how the whole situation had developed. Given my condition, coupled with the relief that we were okay, my father actually went pretty easy on me. He only spoke his ever-applicable saying: "You dopey bastards, you could have died out there." Sure he was glad that I was safe, but it just wasn't his way to express such feelings. I recovered from my ordeal after a few days in bed, and life went on.

Staten Island, New York
1970's

Quietly troubled after his 13 months of service as a Marine in Vietnam, my brother Fred tried to make his way back into the normalcy he had once known. Fortunately, he had returned unscathed, at least in the physical sense of the word. He had seen a good deal of combat and, like so many others, was lucky to be alive. He served his last few months with the Marine Corps in Quantico, Virginia. After his discharge from what he affectionately referred to as "the crotch," he let his hair grow long and grew a beard (as was customary in the early 1970's), and he partied every chance he got. He married shortly after his return and regained the job with the Bell Telephone Company in New York City that he had held before the service. He just always seemed preoccupied by something other than the workaday world.

Upon my own return from Vietnam, I found my brother and most of my friends to be almost unrecognizable, in their behavior as well as their looks. It was as though they had become different people – celebrating, partying, and reveling in good times, all the while trying to shake off the evils of war. For Fred, war had been the catalyst to forever alter his life. Seeking relief from an internal turmoil, he was unable, as were Annie and I, to escape the clutches of the curse; it was a troublesome tenant, an unwanted squatter, which simply resided within our beings. Fred found his job with the phone company to be unfulfilling and, after a prolonged union strike, began to feel the need to move on to something else. Having always been fond of literature, he decided to go back to school to gain the knowledge of those things that he felt would bring him greater happiness. He attended a small college on Staten Island where he found the academic world much to his liking. He enjoyed learning, debating, and exploring the world of formal education.

Outspoken in public and in his writing, Fred quickly developed a reputation for being a strong advocate for veterans' rights. He also became active with the antiwar veterans groups on campus and began to help organize demonstrations, both locally and in Washington, D.C. On one occasion he called me in need of a ride to Valley Forge, Pennsylvania, to join some thousands of antiwar veterans who were gathering there. Valley Forge was the rallying point for people in the Northeast; from there, they would be transported via bus to Washington for a major antiwar demonstration. Fred was with my good friend Bob Hegler, who also shared our curse. In consideration of the fact that they were both wasted, I reluctantly agreed to drive them to Valley Forge; but, despite their repeated requests, I declined to participate in the demonstration.

As much as I had mixed feelings regarding the war, I had not yet given up on it. I knew from my own experience what it felt like to be in a combat zone far from home while there were people condemning your commitment to fight. I remembered being in the middle of Cambodia – fighting for my life – while the Kent State demonstrations took place. It was a sad event. Those demonstrations reverberated through the jungles of Cambodia and Vietnam 10,000 miles away. Still, I felt we needed to win the fight. We had an obligation to honor the sacrifices of those who had fought and either lost their lives or returned home maimed or traumatized for life.

I picked up Fred and Bob, stuffed their sleeping bags and backpacks (along with their bottles of cheap wine and blackberry brandy) into my Volkswagen beetle, and set off for Valley Forge. They were both already really ripped. They sang, drank, smoked pot, and denounced the war throughout the two-hour trip. By the time we arrived, it was late in the night; we drove blindly through the park until we finally happened upon the rallying point. My headlights illuminated the crowd; there were thousands of people, both young and old – hippies all. Most donned their old military clothing as they milled around in the darkness. American flags and banners protesting the war were everywhere – it was quite a sight.

Our progress through the park was considerably slowed as the road we were following was clogged with cars and those on foot. By this time I was anxious to get both of my passengers out of the car. I loved them and their dedication to their cause, but their manic revelry for two hours in the small confines of a Volkswagen was a little bit more than I could take. My patience was wearing thin, and we didn't know exactly where in the park we were going. Then my brother Fred suddenly shouted out, "Up there! That's where we are going. That's the place where we can register." Happy to have reached their destination and ready to get their rally underway, they exited the car. As they gathered their belongings, their empty bottles clanked out of the car and into the street. I bid them well with a handshake and a peace sign. I told them to be careful as they disappeared into the welcoming throngs of antiwar protesters. In a way, I felt bad that I was not going with them as I knew they were in for an adventure, but it was not an adventure that I felt right about joining.

As I exited the park and witnessed the long stream of arrivals intent on going to D.C., I sensed a great wave of determination amidst this assembling sea of jubilant youth. Drawn together in unification against the war and the subsequent toll that was paid in human life, they trumpeted a solitary message: to bring an end to the war in Vietnam. I thought it fitting that Valley Forge should be their point of departure. Several hundred years earlier, this very place had been the scene of contention with an army of citizen soldiers forced to endure a harsh winter while at odds with many of their fellow colonists as to the legitimacy of their own conflict. Then, as now, the momentum of war, once begun, was very difficult to subdue. As each day I relived the glaring reminders of what had been (and what continued to be) sacrificed, I clearly understood the need for this painful war to end. I wondered sadly if, by chance, it was all in vain.

My ride home was much more peaceful without my beloved revolutionaries. They managed to get to Washington, D.C., and were arrested shortly thereafter along with many of their compatriots. Once bailed out, they continued demonstrating until burnt out by their heartfelt disagreement with the war. Exhausted – yet satisfied that their efforts were purposeful – they eventually boarded buses for the return trip. Along with tens of thousands of veterans and civilians alike, they had made a statement that could not be overlooked: We needed to end the war in Vietnam.

***

In a world filled with children who adore their mothers, it is hard to claim that anyone's mother somehow rises above all the rest. Each mother lays claim to bringing forth life, the greatest of human experiences. Acting as a surrogate for the Creator Himself, each mother (in her own way and to varying degrees) shares love, protection, warmth, support, and hopes for the future. Each mother wants her children's lives to be better than her own so that they can appreciate the goodness of life and perhaps one day feel the joy of bringing forth yet another generation. But if, indeed, there were a hierarchy of successful mothers – of those who have upheld and expressed the quintessential ideals of motherhood – then my mother would undoubtedly rank in the category of the highest degree.

My mother's life was selfless: she was devoted to her family, loving, forgiving, kind, generous, and filled with optimism, laughter, and encouragement. She did not live the easiest of lives, but she would not be the one to tell you so. She was not bitter about her lot in life. She learned early to accept the things she could not change; it was a hard-learned philosophy that helped to put her impoverished childhood during the Depression into perspective. She had an optimism, determination, and resourcefulness that were critical to surviving hard times. She saw things as they were, but also as they could be.

Finding pleasure in those simple things life has to offer all of us, regardless of our circumstances, she would say that just a simple hot cup of tea could change your day. If you were fortunate enough to have some milk and a bit of sugar for your tea, then the world was a wonderful place. If, by chance, a slice of toast and a modest bit of jam accompanied your tea, then your troubles could be put on hold if just for some few sips and some small nibbles. She was fond of Irish songs and sayings, many from anonymous authors. I recall one of her favorites was "A deep breath of early morning spring air, a warm embrace, the sun upon your face, and a loving smile. A kind word, a soft breeze, the priceless joy of the laughter of young children – each rivals the riches of the wealthiest man. Hold dear these, the smallest of joys. Let them not become lost in the repetition of our days."

The circumstances of my mother's childhood had brought about an early understanding of the ways of those who were cursed by drink. She had been schooled well in the ways of dealing with the afflicted. She knew what they were capable of, how to communicate with them when drunk, how to limit the suffering they would unwittingly cause themselves and others around them, and when to get out of their way. My mother had helped many a cursed soul to recover after a binge, while listening to their empty assurances that it would never happen again. She knew all too well that no one stopped drinking until they were ready – and they were never ready until they reached their respective bottoms. All the words under the sun are mute to the ears of those cursed; they are deafened by the screams of addiction. Those not close to the cursed will cry that a lack of willpower is their problem, insisting they are weak and have no self-respect. My mother knew the simple truth was that the cursed were powerless over alcohol, and so she never stood in judgment. She was a remarkable woman.

At the age of 53, after having raised a family and with her husband retired (and driving her crazy at home), my mother finally decided to do something for herself: to go back to school. It was a delightful escape. Years prior, her high school education had been cut short when she dropped out to secure work to fulfill the promise to get her siblings out of St. Joseph's Home. She now managed to earn her high school diploma, immediately applied for entry into college, and was accepted by the College of Staten Island. Despite her age and the sometimes awkward interaction with younger students, she quickly found school to be a place she enjoyed and felt comfortable. Moving steadily ahead (as she did with all things), she completed the four years of study to earn a degree in psychology. We were all quite proud of my mother and shocked, but not surprised, some months later when she announced that she had been accepted into the graduate program for secondary school counseling. She landed a job as a high school crisis counselor before she even had her master's degree in hand. Fearless, as always, my mother embarked on her new career at the age of 62.

"Hey, Dad, Charlie is here." Charlie S. was one of the regulars at our house who, as fate would have it, lived only two blocks away. A bricklayer by trade, he was a fun-loving guy who always carried a complex expression of anger, joy, and friendliness that seemed to oscillate across his face. Oftentimes, in conversation, he would throw his head back and to the side with a corresponding, "Oh!" It was his characteristic response to whatever he was hearing or saying, his means of acknowledging the thoughts coming or going from his mind.

He had endured a tough childhood and an even tougher adult life after he was married and became a full-blown alcoholic. Having served in the Marine Corps, Charlie had a respect for discipline and strong leadership; he found these qualities in my father. Mean Mike was known to be a no-nonsense kind of guy, and that was exactly why Charlie wanted (needed) him as his AA sponsor. As time went on, like my father, Charlie had adopted a variety of sayings to deal with life as seen by the addicted mind of an alcoholic. The saying that always stuck with me was "As screwed up as you might be, you are still allowed to have good things come into your life." It was the way he said it that made the expression so poignant; it was obviously a revelation of which he had direct knowledge from his own life experience.

Charlie visited more frequently than most of my father's charges through the years. In fact, Charlie so respected and appreciated my father that he managed to keep his memory and work with AA alive for 20 years after his passing, all the way up until his own death.

My father had a similarly strong friendship with the person who first introduced him to AA back in 1959. That man's name was Kenny D. Kenny was one of our neighbors in the South Beach projects. He worked with my father in the construction industry; oftentimes, on their way to a job site, they would ride the ferry together to Manhattan. In conversation, Kenny shared with my father that he had been in AA for some time and acknowledged that it had changed his life. After suffering a severe concussion, courtesy of yet another drunken brawl, my father was offered a word of advice from a neurologist suggesting the long-term effects of his continued traumas; it was then that he saw fit to ask Kenny if he could accompany him to an AA meeting. The rest was history.

They had shared many adventures together over the years, but one in particular seemed to personify my father's psyche. It took place in the later years of their friendship; at that point in time, my father was in his 70's, and Kenny was in his 80's. Recalling that his friend was "too damn cheap" to pay for a cab to the Staten Island Ferry at the tip of Manhattan, they wound up in the dark caverns of the notoriously dangerous subway system beneath the streets of New York City late one night.

My father had become concerned while they waited in the deserted station. Before long his fears were realized; there appeared a group of young thugs who my father felt were sizing them up for a quick and easy robbery. Always street-smart, he prepared his friend as the group made their way closer by saying, "Get ready to fight." As the apparent threat closed in on them, they heard the reassuring screech of the train on its approach to the station. My father and Kenny quickly boarded the train and found their way to a seat in the empty car. The young thugs followed closely behind and sat directly across from them. Sitting face-to-face, and sure that a confrontation was imminent, my father anticipated the thugs would make their move at any moment. He put on the best war face he could conjure up. He whispered to Kenny that he was going to jump right at the biggest guy in the group, hit him with the bag of apples he was carrying, and bite him in the throat. You had to hear the story being retold to fully appreciate the anxiety of these two old men in such a potentially dangerous situation. Personally, I was not surprised that my father would, in fact, pursue such a tactic. Preparing mentally to strike, he positioned himself ever so slowly for his attack on the swaying train: he steadied his feet to ensure his lurch would be a good one and pressed one hand against the seat. After choosing his target, his adrenaline surging, he realized (to his immediate horror) that he didn't have his teeth in. Lacking his teeth was not advantageous to his bite plan; his gums would not be the deadliest of weapons. And so, without his most basic weapon of desperation, my father remained seated, forced to stand down. The two old men had to rely on a stare down that probably puzzled the young thugs more than anything else. They asked, "What the fuck are you two old bastards looking at?" Both sides were content to offer some insults to each other before the stop for the ferry finally arrived. My father and Kenny exited the train, none the worse for wear, offering the thugs a final sendoff of "Fuck you."

They continued their journey home amidst my father's profane tirade: "You cheap fuck. You could've gotten us both killed by taking that goddamned train." Regardless of how angry my father was that night, his friend Kenny could never really do any wrong in his eyes. Kenny had, after all, put him on the road to redemption.

***

It had been some time since I stopped drugs completely, and it finally felt as though I was coming out of the fog. I was shaken awake by something deep inside myself that sought to be expressed. I once again became aware of the self within me that I had been ignoring; the thing that connected me with the rest of Creation. I needed to understand what life was truly all about. *Was I merely human, or was I more – perhaps a mortal apprentice here to spread peace amongst my fellow man?* So began my life as a seeker.

Despite my drug-laced lifestyle after my discharge from the military, I had managed to work part-time as a housepainter to afford attendance at a community college on Staten Island. One day, during a particularly tedious class on economics, I just felt compelled to get up and leave. I could not see the value of what I was learning there and decided, instead, to engage my efforts in full-time independent study where I could spend my time discovering what was truly important in life. I immersed myself in the worlds of psychology, religion, philosophy, mysticism, and meditation in hopes that I could gain some answers to the troubling questions about life that now dominated my thoughts.

Outside of discussions about AA, conversations around the table with my father typically regarded philosophy, comparative religions, and metaphysics. I had grown up surrounded by books written by and about such fascinating people as Kahlil Gibran, P.D. Ouspensky, George Ivanovich Gurdjieff, and Edgar Cayce. My goal still unclear, my new home became the college library. I had taken the first step on my path as a seeker. I was not sure exactly where I was headed, but I felt sure, nevertheless, there was something deep inside of me that I had to reach. Here in this library I had access to an incredible amount of knowledge and earthly experience before me in these very books; surely amidst this impressive empirical collection I would find what I was looking for.

I felt deep inside that I needed only follow my instincts in this search to, sooner or later, unearth the answers that would satisfy my thirst for meaning in this life. I felt as though I was confronting my existence, challenging everything I knew and bringing my conscious awareness to focus on consciousness itself. Those who have taken such a journey within themselves know it is one of solitary commitment.

My religious upbringing as a Catholic gave me a foundation for belief in a Creator, but my sense of connection to that Creator had been clouded by clerics who chose "faith" as a blanket explanation to put off inquiring minds. I felt it was now my responsibility to search for nirvana, to embark on my own personal crusade to the holy land. The information I could learn and direction I could garner from those who shared a similar journey would serve as my guideposts.

My quest for knowledge, although a laudable endeavor, was looked upon as insane by all who knew me. After all, who quits college to go and study on their own every day at a library in pursuit of something they could not fully explain. My good friend John stopped by to check on me one day to express his concern: "Wow, man, what's going on with you? We don't see you around anymore. Are you okay? Are you mad at us for something?" I assured him that all was well between me and my brothers; I was just pursuing something that was helping me to stay straight. He told me that I could still hang out with them even if I didn't want to get high; but, as he said those words, I could see in his eyes he knew as well as I did that would be an impossible feat. The word amongst my friends was "Moynihan has lost it." That was typically our choice of words for politely saying that someone had gone crazy.

My friends and I had witnessed such behavior before in our neighborhood. A few years back there was a well-liked, good looking, and clean-cut kid by the name of Victor Enzo who had gotten really screwed up and "lost it." Sadly, he had become a meth addict. Then one night he decided to start reading the Bible cover to cover; some years later he became a minister. None of us could believe what had happened to him...and now all eyes were on me to see what would develop in my case. Crazy or not, I was determined to pursue my path. It was hard for me to literally disconnect myself from guys I grew up with, as I knew they didn't understand what I was going through; but it just had to be. I had to follow my instincts.

I became a fixture in the college library. Everyone who worked there knew me. I always studied at the same table; in fact, I spent so much time there that I would get upset if, by chance, someone else was sitting in (what I saw as) my spot. Each day was filled with the words of philosophers, poets, mystics, holy men, and sacred scriptures from which I sought knowledge and inspiration. I felt blessed to be able to spend my time immersed in the sea of knowledge that awaited all those willing to venture out upon it in exploration. I would often read until I fell asleep; on more than one occasion I was roused from my unexpected slumber by the librarian, telling me that they were closing and it was time to go home.

Six months later I had concluded that life was "a sublime torment." Sublime is this Creation in all its consequent wonder; the search for the Creator and our true selves can be a torment. My thoughts went on to suggest that a state of happiness – a cosmic euphoria akin to the greatest state of joy I had ever experienced – could be maintained as a permanent part of my consciousness. There were many paths to reach a life of enlightenment, of a fully realized bond with our Creator; one has only to find the best direction suited to their nature, pursue it with devotion and respect, and hopefully realize their universal status in this earthly life. Enlightenment is a worthy pursuit, even if the final goal is not fully achieved in our allotted time.

Who amongst us has not sought out something beyond ourselves, either for support or perhaps in condemnation? Our preoccupations with the illusions of life leave us distracted from the true nature of Creation in which we are all invested. We exist like a leaf unaware that it is also the tree. We are not forsaken, lost, or abandoned on our journey in this life, only unaware of the truth of Creation that lies before us in an ever-changing world. We are all joined in a great cosmic process, a pilgrimage of seekers and lost souls making our way through our own uncharted regions of Creation. Experiencing the love and pain of our Creator and wanting to know Him better, I was intent to learn, grow, and map the steps that might lead to some answers to the burning questions that have always drawn man to the abstract of some higher power.

Unaware of the incremental steps of evolution in which we amble, I determined that we find ourselves a part of a living equation that has no limits, no solution, and no end – only change. To be considered, we (the equation) must be viewed from outside of ourselves. I found that knowing God and knowing about God were the sole options in a spiritual pursuit. Having read so much descriptive literature, I could quote His words, worship Him, and live life in service to Him and His Creation; but I learned that in itself would not bring about the true conscious and personal connection with God that I sought. I had invited Him into the home of my awareness, and my love was true; but until He became my resident companion – inseparable and merged into my consciousness – I would not fully and truly know Him.

***

Laudable goals, worship, morals, and common beliefs are shared between all great religions; they bring us a way to understand life, maintain order, and enhance our optimism. Sometimes, they even show us a means to find God in our own way. One has only to choose from the wealth of gods who preside over this world in which their influence is paramount, albeit hidden from all in plain view. Many seekers have more questions than answers. Like most of them, I have always found that faith alone as a means of resolving the complex is self-delusional, but to completely set faith aside brings frustration to the most basic and noble endeavor in our lives: realizing God. The comfort that comes from feeling secure in a blanket perception of a Creator can dampen an active, deeper pursuit of who we are. We have but a short time on this earth and want to use our precious moments wisely. We all want to feel that ours is the correct – the only – way to see life; so deep is the desire for some to be connected and engaged in the process of salvation that they will forsake all ideas but their own.

I have always sought a simple understanding of the complexities of Creation, God, and my place in this infinite world. I have embarked on a quiet, addictive pursuit of truth that exists not in the world of word or deed but in the stillness that lies deep beneath both. I've sought to know of consciousness in its purest form throughout my life. My study and contemplation have brought me to understand how right and rewarding it is to seek a true relationship with God. Each of us has a distinctive way of expressing and understanding our shared connection. Life, while complex, is much simpler than we realize.

***

Throughout my time of independent study, I found myself strongly drawn toward the Eastern philosophers of India, the

Vedas, and the life of the holy men known as the Rishi's (the Seers). At one point I read a book called *The Autobiography of a Yogi* based on the life of Paramahansa Yogananda. I knew then that all religions were seeking the same things: the worship of the Creator of this unfathomable, wonderful, and magical universe and to experience the expanse of His fullness in our daily lives along with our individuality. In the course of my reading, I found a passage that related to seekers; it prophesized that if one sought long and wholeheartedly for guidance, a teacher would undoubtedly appear. One morning, as I headed to the library with my coffee in hand, ready to start another day at "Moynihan University," I came upon a poster that would change my life. It announced an introductory lecture on the practice of Transcendental Meditation. Gracing the poster was a picture of Maharishi Mahesh Yogi, wearing a garland of flowers and a warm expression that invited my curiosity. Beneath the picture was a simple message: "The world is as you are. Develop unbounded awareness and the universe will be yours." I was captivated by the simplicity of the message and felt the need to investigate further. I planned to attend the lecture, armed with my skepticism and all the questions I needed to have answered.

Well known internationally as a writer and guru of corporate heads, political figures, and even the Beatles in the late 1960's, Maharishi Mahesh Yogi was a Hindu monk who had left the life of a recluse in the Himalayas to share his insights with the world. It was 1974, and his message of world peace through meditation – without changing one's beliefs, simply by meditating for 20 minutes twice a day – had gained a following of millions worldwide. He had developed a practice of meditation (with origins in a long tradition of Hindu masters) that was applicable to everyone, regardless of their religion or social standing. It was a truly universal means of creating peace on earth. He stated, simply, that a peaceful earth could only be achieved when it is filled with peaceful individuals, and that it is through making each person happy that a happy world would logically follow. The skeptic in me felt it all seemed too simple somehow.

I attended a lecture and listened intently as the instructor gave an overview of Transcendental Meditation (TM). I tried all the while to maintain a healthy skepticism about the information being presented. When the instructor asked if anyone had any questions, my hand immediately shot up. I dominated the question-and-answer period well past the time the lecture was scheduled to end. Satisfied that the information presented was credible and to my liking, I decided to attend another lecture where the necessary steps to learn the practice of TM would be presented. I attended several more lectures before deciding to begin the practice myself. These later lectures were held in the basement of an old home on Staten Island. The homeowner supported TM and provided the space for the local TM teachers to hold their meetings. On the day I was to be instructed, I was told that I would witness an ancient ceremonial recitation called a puja (which would be sung in the liturgical language of Sanskrit). In keeping with ages-old tradition, I was asked to bring some flowers, fruit, and a piece of white cloth to the ceremony.

I had been experimenting on my own for some time with different ways of gaining insight into my own consciousness and its connection to all other consciousness. I had met with varying degrees of success but always felt that something was missing. I knew that I needed someone to show me the techniques necessary to achieve an insight into the different levels of the mind. I found the ceremony of the puja to be a mysterious experience. After the ceremony I was given a mantra and instructed in the proper technique for using it. From the first time I meditated with my mantra, I was convinced I had found something fruitful. And so it was that I practiced the technique for the required 20 minutes twice a day, using my mantra together with a simple ancient procedure to bring my mind to a more subtle state of consciousness. Over time, through repetition and practice, I could see that meditation would heighten my awareness and help me to come into alignment with the laws of nature, to find the true consciousness I had been seeking.

Eventually, word got out to my friends about what I was doing. Having stopped partaking in drugs had been one thing, but becoming a meditator was something completely different. At first they saw it as a novelty, but later they would tell me that they felt I had been brainwashed and was going off the deep end. Amidst all of their condemnation, and mostly out of curiosity, many of them eventually tried it for themselves. Their perception was not on the same level as mine because of their skepticism, but they could see there was some merit to what I was doing and, therefore, kept most of their future insults, evaluations, and sarcasm to themselves.

***

In our Christian traditions we celebrate men and women who we define as saints, those whose lives were somehow out of the ordinary and, in a word, holy. In our Western culture we often overlook (or regard as a curiosity) those individuals of the Far East with a long history of embodiment of the finer qualities of man; however, the Dalai Lama of Tibet, with teachings related to Buddhism, and some lesser-known, Hindu-based spiritual leaders of India have appreciably engaged the world of man, encouraging them to experience God in their lives. Upholding, projecting, and living what we would call "holy" lives, their efforts to improve the life of man were unselfish, devoted, and relentless. Such was the case with Maharishi Mahesh Yogi, an unassuming and remarkable human being with a distinctly pious presence. He had a purity of spirit and a desire for all of humanity to realize their full potential and achieve an ultimate realization of God, however one might perceive Him.

While in the military I had found myself in the presence of many powerful people, true leaders of men with commanding natures. Maharishi Mahesh Yogi not only possessed a similar commanding nature, but he emanated a dynamic spiritual vibration capable of enlivening a deep inner peace within those in his presence. To be in his company always brought me to another place; he was quite literally surrounded by a warm and peaceful yet powerful air. A warrior of the ancient Vedic traditions of which he was a descendent, he carried out a battle against the pervasive ignorance of mankind on a global scale. In the colorful and dramatic depictions of the ancient Vedic texts of India, their holy men were ushered about in golden chariots drawn by mythical steeds. In keeping with the modern age, Maharishi embraced technology and traveled around the world by air; never before had a monk taken to the skies so frequently. He traveled by jet and helicopter, light years away from the cloistered Himalayan environs where he had spent decades studying with his own teacher in the process of unfolding his deepest self. Maharishi circled the world with a message of hope and peace, a blueprint for improving the lives of man.

As he held a degree in physics, Maharishi sought to explain consciousness in terms of science, specifically in terms of quantum mechanics. He would parallel his message of peace to the unified field theory, a theory which investigates the finest levels of material existence by venturing beyond what lies at the source of relative phenomena. Speaking with love and conviction, and always patient with those who challenged his teachings, he served mankind modestly and selflessly.

Inspired by Maharishi, I turned my focus decidedly toward the spiritual aspects of life. Spiritually malnourished and hungry for more understanding, I read his books and attended his lectures. I began to feel the vigorous inspiration I had long been craving. I found great understanding in simple quotes from Maharishi, like this one from his book *The Science of Being and the Art of Living*: "Experience shows that being is the essential, basic nature of the mind; but since it commonly remains in tune with the senses, projecting outwards toward the manifest realm of Creation, the mind misses or fails to appreciate its own essential nature, just as the eyes are unable to see themselves." Before long I was a dyed-in-the-wool meditator. After reading a popular book in the 1960's called *Diet for a Small Planet* (that centered on the inefficiencies of feeding cattle large amounts of grain to produce a pound of beef and suggested that we consume the grain instead), I also became a committed vegetarian. It was a sign of the times: I was a rebellious reformer seeking out those things that would improve my life and my planet.

En route to California
1970's

Things seemed to move quickly for me at that time in my life. Coupled with my impulsive nature and the seeming alignment of my stars, it wasn't long before I was off to California to get a look at a new university established by Maharishi – Maharishi International University, to be exact. To my initial surprise, it was fully accredited, which meant I could apply my veterans' benefits to cover the cost. I was told that the curriculum included meditation classes and courses of study that were given in block form; students could work on one discipline at a time, devoting all of their energy there instead of struggling with several courses of study at once. The idea appealed to me; and, as quick as you could say, "Let's go!" I was off to California.

As fate would have it, my good friend Bob Hegler needed to go to California to see the surgeon who had worked on his injuries after his return from Vietnam. Come to think of it, most of my friends who went to Vietnam were, in fact, wounded; but Bob's injuries had been the most severe. He was shot up pretty badly in the face and in both elbows, which he lost. It was his elbows that the surgeon in Chico, California, would be replacing for him. The Veterans Administration had entrusted Bob with the delivery of the elbows themselves; they were "titanium, of course," as he would say. Although retired from the service and despite his great distance from our home in New York, Bob had somehow managed to secure this surgeon to perform the operation. And so, riding in his big yellow minivan, we accompanied each other to California.

Our trip had sprung up out of nowhere that January; before I knew it, we were on the road. Bob's van was new but not insulated; and so, despite our army surplus sleeping bags, we froze our asses off each night as we were literally living in the van on our trip. We moved across the country state by state, stopping in countless national state parks along the way. Our travel was somewhat spartan; we cooked our own food and bathed when we could. An unfortunate part of our trip was that it was taking place during the oil embargo of 1974, which made it difficult to get gas at times. On more than one occasion, while riding on fumes, I thought we would wind up stranded on some desolate road in the middle of the night. Our modest hardships aside, the trip was terrific. Bob, who I always felt to be the quiet intellectual of my friends, was a great travel companion. Always within arm's reach of a good book and constantly reading, he could talk for hours on virtually any subject. Bob had learned to meditate shortly before we left, and so we practiced the art together each day. We spent long periods discussing our lives' consciousness and Creation. I couldn't have found a more open, intelligent, and spiritual partner with whom to share this adventure.

We were in no rush to get to California; neither of us had a timetable. We enjoyed each other's company and reveled in our shared admiration for the beauty that lies within this great country. It was a great period of peace that we both experienced. It was as though we shared a unique appreciation for living and for this country after fighting as its representatives in Vietnam.

After about a month, we reached the welcomed warmth of the West Coast in Chico, California. His titanium elbows in hand, Bob met with his doctor and scheduled his surgery for the spring. Our next destination would be Mexico, an impromptu stop we had decided to add to our itinerary during the course of our drive to California. On our way south, we stopped at my Uncle Joe's home outside of Los Angeles. I had never spent much time with my mother's brother, but I had always found him to be a pleasant and upbeat guy. Along with my mother, he had bore the brunt of the responsibilities of raising their siblings when they were children. We stayed with him and his wife for several days, enjoying the comforts of a home and a bed. When we mentioned our plan to go to Mexico, he immediately gave a thumbs-down response. After retiring from the Air Force, Joe had worked in the security business. In the course of his work there, he had heard a number of stories (which he now shared with us) regarding long-haired gringos traveling through Mexico and ending up in a small town jail on a bogus charge only to remain imprisoned until a ransom was paid to the local sheriff. In a nice but emphatic way he told us, "Take my advice. Don't go south." His conviction, tone, and serious demeanor swayed us from the random trip through the Third World country. I was disappointed that we would not be seeing Mexico but felt that the uncertainty of our safety was cause enough to seek another destination. We made a compulsory trip to Tijuana, but it took only one day in that cesspool of a city to realize that our travel time would be better spent elsewhere. So uncomplicated was our freedom of choice at the time that we decided to do a 180° and set our sights on Alaska. Spring wasn't too far away, and we figured that by the time we worked our way up the coast and across Canada, it would be a relatively warm journey. We bid Uncle Joe farewell and headed to our next scheduled destination: Santa Barbara, to visit Maharishi International University (MIU).

***

Our trip was a time of healing for both of us. There was a great awakening of spiritual consciousness amidst the proliferation of drugs and wild promiscuous behavior that typically characterized the 1970's in America. The Vietnam War was not yet over, and its trauma was still an open wound in our minds. Every day Bob lived with the painful physical reminders of his combat experience; we both shared the psychological scarring so common among veterans. Our undirected, free-flowing travel gave us the liberating and therapeutic freedom necessary to help ease the stress we had unwittingly sought to assuage with drugs and alcohol since our repatriation some few years earlier. The chronic memories of war are like a song playing in your mind that you can't silence no matter how hard you try. There is an old saying by Michel De Montaigne: "Nothing fixes something in your memory more than trying to forget it." We reached the point where we could finally speak of our time in Vietnam. At times we would share the stories of the evils we had experienced; it seemed as if each time a story was reluctantly shared, the painful memory would be ever so slightly diminished.

Bob and I were like so many others who had been charmed by the adventure that cloaked the true essence of war from the young. It had enticed our youthful minds with the grand visions of battles, victory, bravery, and trials that young men seek. Once stripped of its façade, however, war had shown itself unashamed, remorseless, and hungry for the souls of those caught up in its perpetual web of death. The threads of that web remained close at hand even for those of us whose souls were spared, forever attached to our beings; if we happened to disturb the mental filaments of that web, the ever-vigilant beast of war promptly confronted us with an evil presence of renewed fear in an attempt to consume yet another piece of our souls. We were forever linked to the source of our pain, anchored to the experience of man's worst legacy.

War served (and continues to serve) as a reminder of how primitive we are as a race despite our self-appointed status and accolades as the most highly-evolved species on this planet. The boundless ego of man does not allow us to long entertain thoughts of how peaceful this planet may be if it lacked our presence; yet I, personally, had to momentarily acknowledge the great unspeakable evil that had been woven throughout our short history here on Earth – the all-too-short periods of peace interspersed with the ongoing battles between good and bad, satiation and desperation, and joy and pain.

As we had learned from experience, war is a fundamental matter of survival. It is a contest between flushing civilizations seeking expansion and domination, often rooted in ideology, economics, and the acquisition of natural resources. *What man would not lay down his life to protect his family, exhausting every effort to ensure their well-being? What man would not stand in defense of the things he cherishes?* Warring without threat or provocation is evil, but to wage war upon those who would themselves kill us is justifiable.

***

Bob and I continued our travels like national tourists, absorbing all we could of the wonders of America along the way. We took great joy in lingering in the plains, the deserts, the Rocky Mountains, and the Pacific coast – they all offered us the best they had in natural beauty. We would often choose to stop and meditate to absorb what nature was so freely offering. This country of ours is, indeed, beautiful.

Before long we reached Santa Barbara and the facilities housing Maharishi International University. I was immediately struck by the sense of peace that seemed to permeate the small campus. I met with the admissions office, discussed the curriculum, gathered applications for the next semester, and talked to as many students as I could to get their insight into the university that was, by all Western standards, in a word, different. "Different" didn't really come anywhere near describing MIU. To begin with, I had never heard of a university in the United States that had its roots in the Vedic traditions of India; much less one led by a holy man who had left the Himalayan Mountains on a quest to spread peace throughout the world. One of the prerequisites to studying at MIU was to begin the practice Transcendental Meditation. It was the practice of TM that established the foundation of this educational process. Together with a core course called "The Science of Creative Intelligence" (SCI), it laid the groundwork for everything else one would learn there. SCI was the theoretical side of learning; it explained the ways in which all disciplines are connected to one another through an understanding of pure consciousness, the basis of all things that find their expression in the relative field of existence. The practical side of learning was achieved through meditation, the actual connection to the experience of the reality of pure consciousness.

I learned about the ground-breaking scientific research that had already been conducted here at MIU. Dr. Keith Wallace, a physiologist at the university, had utilized sophisticated equipment to measure the brain activity of those in a meditative state. He discovered a pattern amidst those who meditated which indicated a unique physiology distinct from those who did not meditate. His findings were published, leading the way for thousands of future studies on the impact of meditation toward individual and societal improvements. These studies were key, as Maharishi was quoted, "to provide a means for scientific verification through measurement and the ability to reproduce the results to validate what was happening before, during, and after meditation."

My initial visit to the facilities also opened up thoughts of the possibility of my becoming a teacher of TM myself. It was a vocation that greatly appealed to me as I considered myself uniquely suited for contributing to Maharishi Mahesh Yogi's cause of world peace. Having participated in war, I felt a strong obligation to contribute, in whatever way I could, to the establishment of peace amongst my fellow man. Maharishi had a plan for a better world, and I believed that teaching his practice would be like being a part of a spiritual Peace Corps.

Once my business at the university was completed, Bob and I reluctantly left Santa Barbara and continued our travels up the Pacific Coast. We jumped on and off the interstate that ran north along the coastline, investigating small towns and state parks along the way. Bob and I agreed that a trip around the country should be part of every college curriculum. We felt there was so much knowledge and experience to be gained by traveling through our country. Connecting with our fellow Americans – those people with whom we shared a pride, a reverence, and a celebrated history – was both enlightening and exhilarating.

For some reason we had the urge to stop and rent a boat to explore Lake Oroville in California. Neither Bob nor I were terribly familiar with boats, but we knew the basics; and so we spent the day exploring the unending series of tributaries and coves around the huge reservoir. We entered into one remote cove and found ourselves slowly venturing further and further into a gradually narrowing passageway lined with trees and huge boulders. Ultimately, we came upon a calm, shallow, and picture-perfect spot where we shut off the engine and decided to meditate. After twenty minutes we opened our eyes to find, to our wonder, that everything around us was covered with large, beautiful butterflies. Coming out of meditation, with the boat bobbing ever so gently, those butterflies provided this spectacular spot with an extra layer of beauty. They were all over, even covering us and our boat. The butterflies were rising and falling silently in delicate waves of color, creating a magical and surreal experience. It was a true gift of nature, one of those beautifully memorable moments capable of displacing some of the darker landscapes of our memory. We lingered there for what seemed to be an eternity, speaking ever so quietly so as not to disturb this incredible vision with the words of man. Eventually feeling the need to move on, we slowly paddled awhile before starting our engine so as not to disturb the serenity of the scene. No one else would ever experience that vision in quite the same way; it was uniquely ours. It is truly remarkable how beautiful this life can be when we allow ourselves to see it simply, through eyes that are clear and free from the turbulence that tends to cloud our perception.

***

Our travels were different now, on somewhat of a timetable as I would be attending MIU in the not-too-distant future. I was still having the time of my life traveling with Bob, but having a goal for the future gave me something tangible to hold onto: a much-needed optimism. Bob had thought about attending MIU himself (and would have surely enjoyed it), but his ongoing schedule of surgeries and inability to communicate clearly forced him to defer. The wounds that had disfigured Bob's facial bones and his tongue when he was shot in the face in Vietnam had greatly impaired his ability to speak. Although I had grown to understand him, most people found it difficult; it was a frustration I could clearly sense whenever he was asked to repeat himself. Not one to complain, he worked his way through his disability as he did with all things.

Bob had once told me that there was a system of preparing for the real world that had developed in the wards of the seriously injured during the two years he spent recovering in the hospital after Vietnam. There was no sympathy available amidst those with disfiguring traumatic injuries. Whether they were missing limbs or brutally burned, they shared a common bond in that they knew they would all be seen much differently than when they embodied the healthy, young physiques of their pre-Vietnam days. They knew that people would now quite possibly divert their eyes once their injuries were realized. Seen as cold by those outside, the meaningful torment of fellow patients in their "club of misfortune" helped each man to develop his own way of becoming hardened. The club was open to all, but there was a terrible price to be paid for membership: they would focus on, not ignore, each others' disabilities. As Bob explained it, if a man had lost a leg, he was told he would never be a dancer; a missing arm would rule him out as a juggler; burns brought a note that he would never win a beauty contest; and on and on went their priming for reentry into society. Those in the club of misfortune were always reminded of who they were – not to limit their aspirations, but to place them in perspective. Bob said it was hard at first, but that it did help him and many others to become comfortable with who they now were and how they would be seen by others in society.

***

So welcoming was our time in the artist-filled coastal towns along the misty and lush green shores of the Pacific Northwest that I felt I could get permanently lost in the peace I felt there. We moved steadily along at a happy pace until we reached Vancouver, Washington, on the Columbia River. Bob was excited to arrive as he had a good friend there. A nurse with whom he had become acquainted during his years in the Army hospital had given Bob an open invitation to stay with her and her husband if ever he was able to come their way. They had recently purchased a big, old Victorian home and had plenty of room. He had called them early in our journey to tell them that he would be on the West Coast. I found them to be wonderful people. So good was our time there that we put Alaska on hold to stay with them for an entire month. Both Bob and I were handy; we spent our days helping them paint and repair their newly-acquired home. Exploration of Mount Saint Helens, Mount Hood, the Seven Sister Mountains, and the Columbia River kept us occupied during our free time. Both Bob and I found peace in these monumental places; they offered a majestic and tranquil environment.

By that time we had been on the road for several months and were growing weary of the thought of the trek to Alaska. It would have been a great adventure but our decided futures seemed to be calling us. For me, meditation, MIU, and the fulfillment of my desire for greater understanding of the spiritual side of life beckoned. For Bob, his health was his main concern as he would continue to have his body rebuilt. When Bob received news that the surgery on his elbows could be performed sooner than expected, we reluctantly decided to part company, ending (what seemed to be) our three-month spiritual odyssey across the United States.

It was a bittersweet moment. I had found our trip to be a truly liberating and healing experience for both of us. Now drawn in different directions, we would bid each other farewell. Bob would work his way back down the coast to Chico, California. I would fly home from Vancouver to New York. I have never known anyone with whom I was as compatible as Bob. I admired his ability to deal with his physical injuries and how – with never a word of anger, condemnation, or self-pity – he was always accepting of whatever life brought his way. I had fallen in love with the West Coast and could certainly have remained there and started a new life, but something called to me from back east. In those days, I usually relied on my gut feeling to give me direction. I did not spend a great deal of time weighing one thing against the other; rather I was impulsive – often to the extreme – as I believed some external force offered me certain guidance.

Flying had always brought me a sense of freedom, of breaking free from earth and leaving behind, if only for a short while, all the troubles that weighed me down. Moving amidst the clouds, feeling somehow closer to the heavens, always seemed to enliven something deep within me. The long flight home gave me time to savor the changes in my life. I felt a great appreciation for my life and for the direction in which I was about to take it.

Staten Island, New York
Early 1970's

Once home, I felt a renewed sense of vitality. I submitted my paperwork to MIU and worked out the financing with the Veterans Administration and the school. I was scheduled to begin my studies in the fall of 1974. Keeping myself clean from drugs, alcohol, and smoking, I worked through the summer in preparation for my move west. My friends treated me with respect despite their continued confusion over the disappearance of the Mickey they once knew. They were still unsure of my behavior but hoped that I was aware of what I was doing and wished me well, even if they thought I was nuts.

Shortly before my scheduled departure, I learned that, since visiting the campus in Santa Barbara some months earlier, The International Meditation Society (the organizing branch of TM) had purchased an entire university in Fairfield, Iowa, and relocated the campus. Having already envisioned myself enjoying the beauty of the West Coast, I was a little disappointed, but undeterred. I was committed to my goal, and so the Midwest would now be my destination.

***

Let it not be said that the Moynihan family was short on ideas that could change the world. Some call it a pie-in-the-sky mentality; but, for us, it was a flow of creativity that was part of our nature. There were periods when we were blinded by our own enthusiasm and the (sometimes irrational) eccentric vision of the creative spirit. My father lived in a world of quiet obsession. Fascinated by the natural world and how things worked, he would always be theorizing or ruminating over something. Like a mad professor, he would stay up into the wee hours of the morning pursuing some idea and writing papers to submit to different government and private organizations as well as to think tanks around the world. His choice of reading material fluctuated between physics and the transcendental. Both the physical and spiritual world pulled at his consciousness, leaving him with one foot in the relative and the other in the clouds. Fueled by Tesla, Einstein, and other like-minded geniuses, he would stretch his abstract thinking into the realm of the metaphysical.

His upbringing as an Irish Catholic gave him a foundation for belief, but it never satisfied his inquisitive minds' search for a more concrete and meaningful experience of God's presence. He was never overtly religious; in fact, he always felt that many who worshiped did so out of fear of what might befall them at the end of this life. He surmised that any God who awaited him after a lifetime on this perilous planet would need to be benevolent, aware of the shortcomings of man and forgiving. Nourishing his spiritual needs were a wide variety of philosophers, spiritual poets, and mystics. He was fond of quoting passages (sometimes familiar, oftentimes obscure) in an attempt to make a point that was, according to him, "thought through by minds greater than his own." His strong insights and reflection seemed an endemic part of his generation; a generation that had survived the Depression, fought for years in World War II, and kept a stiff upper lip (as the English would say) all the while trying to stabilize, or at least endure, the tumultuous internal workings of humankind during that era.

With a creative and inquisitive mind, my father would entertain all manner of new inventions, including a few of his own. One in particular had its origins in the work of the physicist Nickolas Tesla. Tesla, fascinated by electricity, had spent most of his life quantifying and manipulating this mysterious unseen force. My father was convinced that electricity could be encouraged to flow freely from the earth itself by introducing current into the ground as a primer to allow for a siphoning effect. Mildly obsessed with the idea, he would regularly blow circuit breakers and scare the hell out of us with his dangerous electrical play. We thought for sure he would one day be electrocuted. Whenever he donned his goggles and thick rubber gloves, we knew he was heading for another experiment. Unfortunately, the earth was never coaxed to give up whatever current it might have possessed. This particular undertaking only resulted in skyrocketing electric bills. It seems to me (now) that his endeavor was more of an exercise than serious science; it was just a way of letting his imagination run wild.

Several monikers followed my father through his lifetime. As we got older, my friends, along with his countless AA charges, affectionately referred to him as "Mean Mike." Six feet tall, with red hair, a wild scowl, and the countenance of a bulldog, he was feared by all of them. To those steelworkers who knew him in the world of construction, where he hung his Irish cap most of his life, he was known as "Iron Mike," partly for his chosen trade but mostly because of his demeanor – he had a glance that could melt ice and an abrupt New York City Way of speaking. My father was someone you didn't want to rub the wrong way. Many people were not fond of him because of his direct, no-nonsense way of communicating, but his thought on that subject was "I really don't give a shit who likes me." His words had a sharp edge, a certain sarcasm that may have had its roots in his Irish heritage. He was a tough man to get to know, and I often wonder if anyone ever really knew him well at all. A hard shell guarded his emotions, keeping his feelings hidden in an impenetrable isolation. He endured that isolation, likely accepting it as his own making.

In the days prior to finding himself through AA, my father had been notorious in our neighborhood. When we left the projects, I'm sure there were many people there who were glad to see him move on. Well-known in the local bars he frequented, it was assumed that whether he came in drunk or sober, trouble of some sort would soon develop. *Insane* was probably the best way to describe him. Far too many fights, with too many blows to the head, and the residual effects of World War II had brought about his unusual persona. Later, in his sober years, he would recount stories that were (from a normal point of view) unlikely and improbable, even unbelievable; yet I knew they were the truth because my father was not one to brag or bullshit. God knows how many stories he had forgotten.

On one occasion, under the influence of John Barleycorn in a crowded bar, he crossed paths with a dog handler who chose to bring his dog – a large German Shepherd – into the establishment. Conspicuous in such a setting, words were exchanged about the dog as the man bragged about how powerful and vicious it was. The man went on for some time about the attack dog's prowess. Eventually, my father cut him short, sarcastically saying over the top of his beer glass, "I could take that dog down without any problem." The owner, shocked by the assertion, bristled and said, "Go ahead, you want to take him on." A betting frenzy erupted amongst the drunken patrons as to who would win in the contest between man and beast. More drinks flowed from my father's supporters while he prepared for his proposed duel with the canine. A crescendo developed as my father downed his last shot, followed by the traditional glass of beer.

The barkeep suspended service and unbolted the door that led to the alley behind the bar, the arena where man and beast would do battle. Pushing off from the bar like a prize fighter leaving his corner, with his fellow patrons in wild anticipation, my father proceeded to the alley for the deadly confrontation. By now even the dog was worked up, sensing that something was about to happen; he was barking, snarling, and pulling wildly at his leash. The rules were set out: there were no rules. The dog would be brought up the alley; and my father, waiting at the other end, would present himself as a conspicuous target and then encourage the dog to advance. The handler would command the dog to attack on a signal. The drunken revelers cheered for the contest to begin as if they were patrons of the Coliseum. "Get him!" the dog handler yelled; in response, the German Shepherd charged my father. Building speed as he ran down the alley, the dog hit him straight in the chest. The two of them went down in a tangle of hair, growls, flashing teeth, and flailing limbs – a more bizarre scene one could not imagine. The crowd went nuts. Already bitten several times in this fight to the death, my father managed to get his legs around the dog's midsection and his arms around its neck. Squeezing ever harder with his legs, the dog was unable to breathe and, in time, became subdued. Realizing what was happening, the owner yelled, "Okay, okay, you win. Let him go, let him go!" Reluctantly, my father released the dog and arose as the victor. Amidst repeated tributes, he brushed himself off and returned to the bar. His clothing ripped and bloodied, this urban gladiator was celebrated with drink late into the night. My father said he couldn't remember where he had picked up his technique for subduing a wild dog; fortunately, he never had the occasion or need to apply it again.

On another, somewhat lighter, occasion my father had returned from work in one of his more inebriated states. I often wondered how he even managed to find his way home sometimes. Usually commuting on public transportation from New York City to the suburbs of Staten Island, he was like a homing pigeon that had some inner sense of direction that seemed to take over, allowing him to return to his nest despite the deadening of all his faculties. On this particular evening, he arrived at our building and made his way to the elevator. He pressed what he thought was the button for the sixth floor; in fact, he had pressed the button for the third floor. Now, the floor plans and apartment layouts were the same for the first through the sixth floors in the projects; so, regardless of what floor one exited, everything appeared identical to the floors above and below. Thus, my father proceeded to make his way to what he thought was apartment 6A; it was actually 3A. Since few people locked their doors back then, he was able to enter the unlocked apartment without issue. He went to the living room and passed out on the couch. Sometime later he was roused by our shocked neighbors and encouraged to move himself up to the sixth floor.

I'm sure they were aware of his volatile reputation and were probably relieved when he moved on peacefully. We only found out about the incident when our young neighbor broadcasted in front of our friends, "Boy, your father was really drunk last night," and then shared that he had been found fast asleep on the couch in their living room. It was a bizarre and humiliating story that drew much laughter and ridicule from our large group of friends. It was also one of those stories that spread quickly and would last in the young, impressionable minds of our friends and neighbors for a long time to come. We young Moynihan's could only endure our father's embarrassing behavior and hope that there wouldn't be another such incident for a while (or that someone else's father would do something even more peculiar).

Fairfield, Iowa
1974

"Fairfield, Iowa? What the hell is going on in Fairfield, Iowa? I thought you were going to Santa Barbara? Who just buys an entire university? I don't know about this." My father's response had been wary when I told him about the new location of MIU. There was an upsurge in nontraditional spiritual and religious groups at that time in our country's history; their charismatic leaders were quickly gaining national and international followings. It was commonplace to see active representatives of those groups on the streets of New York City. The Moonies (a name derived from their founder, Sun Myung Moon) sold flowers on street corners to raise money for their leader. Their preoccupied expressions provided a window into their organization's indoctrination; they were zombie-like and near impossible to engage in conversation. The Hare Krishnas, on the other hand, were joyful in their revelry. Donning robes and shaved heads, they would be seen in groups, gathered to dance and sing the praises of the Indian god Krishna. There were many other such groups – some altruistic, others predatory.

"Don't be buying any wooden nickels," my father warned. He had seen the positive effect that meditation had on me and, given his own interest in metaphysics, was open-minded; yet his cautious nature prompted him to ensure I knew what I was getting into. I respected his concern and assured him I had vetted the organization thoroughly over the last year. I felt confident in this international group that had established their credibility with large corporations, celebrities, and millions of followers world-wide. Maharishi Mahesh Yogi sincerely sought to bring world peace and enlightenment to the masses through the practice of Transcendental Meditation.

When the time for my departure arrived, I bid my family farewell, excited to begin this new journey in my life. I was hopeful that it would fulfill my expectations of providing a greater insight into the meaning of life and the tools needed to sculpt out my place in this Creation. My flight to Iowa was filled with thoughts of what I might find once I arrived. Landing not far from Fairfield, in the town of Ottumwa, my first thought was *my God, this place is flat.* I passed one farm after another on the bus ride from the airport. It occurred to me that one of our country's greatest blessings was its ability to produce vast quantities of food. The Midwest was certainly a "bread basket," and it would now be my new home.

Once on campus, I made my way to the admissions building and joined the line of incoming students – seekers all. The freshman class was small by most standards, only 400 people. My fellow students seemed to be from everywhere in the country. We were a mesh of urban and rural youth connected by our practice of Transcendental Meditation. I struck up a conversation with the guy behind me on line and was shocked by our exchange. It turned out to be one of those chance meetings that were almost unbelievable. I asked, "Where you from?"

"California," he said, "San Jose. How about yourself?"

"New York," I replied.

"No kidding? I grew up in New York. On Staten Island."

"No way! That's where I'm from. Staten Island. What's your name?" I asked with piqued interest.

"Jim Rocca."

"I'm Mickey Moynihan."

"The name 'Moynihan' sounds familiar. Where did you go to school?"

"I went to St. Sylvester's."

He looked at me in disbelief as he said, "That's where I went to school. I was in your brother Fred's class."

We stood there in shock as we tried to process what was taking place. There are eerie moments in life where coincidence leaves us dumbfounded. For me and Jim Rocca, this was one of those moments. In the short while we waited on that line in the middle of Iowa, we established a permanent bond. Both of us sensed the unique rarity of our chance encounter. For two people who went to school together thousands of miles away and many years ago, to be reunited as we both searched for better lives through the practice of meditation seemed to be somehow by design – fated.

Jim and I shared another bond, regarding our military service. Unknown to either of us until this current meeting, we had both been stationed in Vietnam in 1970, serving at the same time and in the same unit. Jim had been a helicopter pilot who ferried troops into combat; we speculated as to whether or not we had actually flown together on any of the many missions in which we had both participated. Like me, Jim carried ghosts from the war. A devastating helicopter crash, close encounters with death, and the exposure of his soul to war brought us even closer in the incomparable and immediate bond experienced between survivors. We would remain close friends from that point onward.

As we continued through the registration process, I found that our encounter brought me a certain comfort; it was good to know that someone who shared a similar background was also pursuing a similar goal. Those enrolling here were from every part of the country and every walk of life. All were in search of something intangible: something more than the knowledge to be garnered from books or the words of man, something more than faith or dogma. We were ardently in pursuit of something that, by attribute of its nature, defies concrete description. We all sought a spiritual maturity in the ongoing experience of the ultimate permeating and connecting force of Creation: pure consciousness.

MIU felt like a new start for me in many ways; here I adopted an optimistic view for the future. It seemed I had left my resume of ills, shortcomings, and disappointments with life back in New York. Leaving behind all that was familiar, with family and friends concerned and unsure of what I was pursuing, I set out to establish a life worth living. I had willingly set out to follow the principles of a former recluse, a holy man who had given up everything to devote his life to his master and the goal of bringing about peace in this world through meditation. The education here was accredited and traditional in nature, but tied to an understanding of the unity of all disciplines as an expression of consciousness. I was fascinated by this approach to learning.

I was also fascinated by the man behind it all. Maharishi Mahesh Yogi had arrived on the world stage in 1959. In keeping with his traditions as a monk, he was an unassuming, small man cloaked in white garments, adorned with long hair and a beard. He had a charming disposition and a bigger-than-life vision of bringing peace to the world one person at a time. Having been tasked by his master with the seemingly-impossible mission of reaching out to all of humanity, he was now recognized around the world for the endeavors he began in the remote areas of northern India.

My first year at MIU was rewarding beyond anticipation. Seeking so desperately to understand this Creation outside of its beautiful and vast trappings, I became engrossed in the fundamental precepts of existence. Along with the rigorous course of study, there were periods of extended meditation that gave rise to personal and unique insights of Creation, bringing greater clarity to the world as viewed through my particular level of consciousness. These periods of introspection, in an environment conducive to such pursuits, allowed for a better understanding of Maharishi's words that had first caught my attention some years earlier: "The world is as you are. Develop unbounded awareness and the universe will be yours." The universe was certainly not yet mine, but I now felt I was invested in a piece of the universal real estate, always reserving some of my mental capital for its growth. I cherished every moment of my new adventure.

Isola, France
Summer of 1976

And then there I was in June of 1976, arriving with a group of 50 MIU students at a three-month TM Teacher Training Course in the French Alps. We were at a resort in Isola, France, several hours north of Nice, on the Italian border. Six thousand feet above sea level and surrounded by snowcapped mountains, the location was clearly chosen for its beauty as well as its remoteness; our environs were serene, removed from the distractions of a busy world. I had the good fortune of sharing the experience with my close friend Jim; together we would delve deeper into ourselves to engage the vast light of truth that dwells within our beings. At the end of our studies, we would be instructors of TM. Our course of study would include the history of TM, the methodology for teaching meditation, and a variety of practical procedures intended to ensure the efficacy of our instruction. It seemed a great culmination to my first year of study – a year that had been filled with new friendships and knowledge, both traditional and esoteric. During this year I had developed a greater respect and admiration for Maharishi and his goal of creating a world at peace; now I would learn to serve as an extension of his outreach to all mankind.

As I entered the hotel where we would be spending the next three months, I felt like I had entered a modern Himalayan retreat. After checking in I found my way to my room and was pleased by the comfort it afforded. The view from the balcony was picture-perfect; it allowed for an ever-changing, weather-driven panorama amidst the mountains. It was here that, for the first time in many years, I felt truly safe – sheltered from the demons in my life that kept me on edge. The painful reminders of war seemed unable to survive at the refined heights in which I now dwelled. If it is possible to gain a geographical escape from life, than this, for me, was the place.

One particularly beautiful evening, while sitting comfortably on the balcony of my room, I settled back in preparation to meditate. In the distance I could hear a mountain stream, fed by melting snow from high above, creating a murmur on its way toward lower elevations. The air, remarkably rarefied, made each weightless breath a gift. Slowly the sky unfurled its hidden stars, allowing their subtle, penetrating rays to stir something deep inside of me. I felt rightly separate from, yet closely connected to everything. It was what I can only describe, in a word, as "serenity" – a deep feeling of how precise everything was in Creation, an inescapable closeness to the infinite design before me. It was a feeling that defied any complete description through words; yet in that suspended moment of reflection, I had an experience unlike any other I had known in my life.

I closed my eyes to meditate and soon found myself in a captivating internal state where I lost absolutely everything – my past, my family, my friends, my possessions; time and all my desires virtually ceased. It was as if my mind had become a clean slate. Life had become transparent, unified in the warmth of consciousness. As all the worldly material things that made me who I was fell away, they were replaced by an unabridged experience of all things in a single moment. In the periphery of my existence, my breathing and heart rate – the two rhythms with which I had been inseparable from birth, the drum beats of my life – were conspicuous by their absence, replaced by a peaceful suspension of activity. Eternity prevailed in that moment.

Like a sunrise, the episode spoke for itself. I entertained a wordless internal dialogue of infinite proportions. We seek – through art, music, literature, and dance – to express such things to others. Historic creations like the pyramids and (to a lesser extent, but no less heartfelt) the cathedrals and stone edifices of ancient cultures share one thing in common: the need to recognize a grand link between ourselves and something greater than words, if not our Creator. Vacillating between the unmanifested and the finest level of the relative, I began to experience the presence of what I felt was God. Not in the anthropomorphic way I had been taught traditionally as a Christian, but profoundly. The experience was consuming in its simplicity as I assimilated into a receptive, enduring light, sending waves of joy throughout the vessel wherein all this was taking place. Like a drop merging with and becoming the ocean, I felt whole. *Who would believe that we could be brought to experience such things through meditation?* My singular consumption of spiritual enchantment was timeless, resistant to analysis. Waning and too quickly over, the experience left a long-standing, though not-often-repeated impression. Like trying to bring to mind a thought that seeks to remain ephemeral, my glimpses of such things were often incidental to the process of meditation.

I would later find myself hesitant to consider the word "God" in conjunction with the experience. I had known far too many distractions within the word. I found, for a time, greater utility in the simple recollection of the subtle phenomena that meditation would provide as a visual reminder, expressive of the continuum of symmetric design, giving rise to and bringing a deeper meaning of the abstract.

During this three-month period, I came to realize the evolutionary challenges one faces in the pursuit of enlightenment. Like a stream of souls, we all flow toward greater levels of awareness. Some move quickly closer to their goals, fully aware of the course nearing termination. Others feel their way forward through the changing landscape of life, merely hopeful of their journeys' end. Many of us are constrained by life's obstacles, those things that can slow our progress by diverting us into swirling pools of distraction. Like a blind man in a grand cathedral, I have felt the echoes of the boundless Creation in all its grandeur, caressing the pillars of the material world. I have borrowed words from minds greater than my own to speak of that great mystery upon which we all must eternally dwell. Inadequate, wanting, are my senses and my intellect to provide the understanding I seek. I feel like a motherless child in my need, seeking to regain a connection to the source of my beginning in a village filled with orphans, none any the wiser. Calling to me from beyond those village walls, which simultaneously protect and confine my life, are the answers I seek; they are being whispered in the dark of night amidst the stars and crying out in the radiance of the sun.

My stay at Isola was an extraordinary spiritual adventure. It provided me with what would be a lifelong companion of understanding (a much more welcome companion than those I had previously acquired in Vietnam). Shortly before I left Isola, I had the profound opportunity to sit shoulder-to-shoulder with Maharishi. It was a moving and privileged experience to speak with him directly. His presence projected the power of nature – immense, beautiful, and peaceful. I was honored to be a part of his world plan of peace through meditation.

Having satisfied the requirements of the course of study and now a teacher of Transcendental Meditation, I reluctantly parted company with my friends and the French Alps to return to the States. Feeling ready to share what I had learned, I began teaching TM around the country. I was always surprised by the broad and diverse appeal TM had throughout society. The young and the old; the wealthy, poor, and middle classes alike; all were drawn by its simplicity of message and practice. I encountered a quiet, waiting populous with a distinctive interest in self-improvement, even if seen as unconventional: some sought greater spiritual insight; some wanted to reduce the stress in their lives; and still others, out of curiosity or just to feel a greater peace. I always felt that those who I taught came away with what they were looking for.

Staten Island, New York
Late 1970's

One of the most intimate moments I ever shared with my father occurred not long after I returned from my cherished journey to France. I knew my father had always held a reserved curiosity about the meditation I practiced. I knew he was unsure of how it worked and whether or not he believed the benefits to be gained were real or imagined. At times he would jokingly refer to me as "hitting the sheets" when I would excuse myself to meditate. But I was now in a position to share with him the things I had learned, the knowledge that I valued. I hoped he would find it useful, if not inspiring.

I knew my father would be more receptive to learning in a place where he was comfortable, so I taught him to meditate at home as opposed to at a TM center. I had talked with him several times in preparation for the initiation ceremony. Once begun, however, I could sense that he was uncomfortable throughout most of the process; he sat with rigid posture and wore a stoic expression. Having shared the technique with him, we meditated for a short while. Although his response to learning the practice of meditation was subdued, he respected the process and appreciated my teaching him. I felt he was not sure how to react to what he had experienced; that was not an unusual response for those first learning TM. In fact, it was the same response my mother had when she eventually learned the process. We never talked about their experiences again. I wondered if they thought I had gone over to the other side – become a Hindu – and would eventually wind up in an Ashram somewhere in the Himalayas. Regardless, I was glad to have started them on the path to meditation.

Beyond the incense, rumination, and affectations of the meditating community, I found there to be a precious wealth of knowledge. Before me was a map that began from where I stood and led to where I could be. As time went on, this Creation felt like an old friend with whom I was reuniting. To be so totally absorbed by something is an experience of exceptional beauty, a journey we can only experience on our own. I had gained some insight, a better understanding, of how someone could devote their entire life in pursuit of a union with God – such a laudable goal, yet hard to conceive in our troubled and materialistic age. It is a course chosen by many throughout recorded history, with results hidden within their own consciousness.

Transcendental meditation and its teachings became my new setting for North and South – a moral, spiritual, and social compass lending direction to my life. I now saw life as a matter of degrees of consciousness. Always being guided, pulled toward a particular destination, by some gentle and unseen force aware of where I was and where I should be heading, my perception of what was occurring around my being was just that: my perception. The joy and the pain were all part of the process, put into context by my individual level of consciousness.

***

Wanting to speak out, I call upon my Creator, but my voice falls short of the strength, courage, and purity needed to carry my words. *And what words are befitting a conversation with one omniscient? From whom have these words originated, and do they have any meaning other than what we use them for here on Earth? Are our words mere sounds or vibrations, reverent in their origin, thankful and humble in expressing what is already known?* Yet I feel the need to call out, to ask my Creator to lighten my load with His presence, if for only a minute; to let it feel like days. Let me grasp a host of millennium and hold them near. "Let me, thy creation, know thee in a relative form that reveals thy greatness to my primitive eyes. Let me, in thy presence, thank thee for my blessings and this Creation. Countless times I have spoken to thee without seeing to whom I speak. If it pleases you, show thyself before your humble child. Let my eyes fill with your glory, and let it radiate through my being. Allow me that which will bring me hope, understanding, and joy in this lifetime. So many seek thy presence, and I am but a heartbeat amidst all things possible. Let my words of longing fall upon a loving ear, and grant me this blessing if I be worthy. Might I speak then for all and ask for those who seek to know thee to shine upon them as well. For how great would my joy be to share thy presence with the rest of the family of man. What a wonderful thing it would be for all of man to stand before thee as thy great cosmic veil is lifted. If only for a moment, thy presence would cleanse our world of pain and ignorance, carrying away forever the errors of man in the winds of purity. Speechless before thee, we could only reach out with an Earth-wide embrace; and cherish the moment in thy arms, hoping it would never end. I call out to thee whom I know like no other and hope, in the simplest of ways, that what I seek might be so. And, if so, may I ask how long the wait might be? I ask only so my heart is not worn from waiting. If it must be one day, one year, or the rest of my life, so be it. For what greater thing could there be than to stand before that which is all? Should my being not be worthy of such a moment, I would likely wither."

Even in contemplation of what I don't know, I sense a weakness, a failing – even a splendid fear. "Do I, your child, speak out of place? Do I presume too much in asking such things of a Father who has given His all? With a loving heart, forgive my thoughts, my words, and my actions if they seem ungrateful. Let me thank thee in advance for whatever is to come. Just through our speaking I already feel thy being enlivening me within: filling me with a special fire that brings hope, love, and knowledge by its presence; and separating me from this moment in which I am connected to thee by the finest of fibers that connects all hearts. A wordless song seeks to burst from my soul, a glowing melody burning without consuming. I am awash in a river of adoration. Shall I call upon the wind to carry my song so all may hear? Or the sun to warm the path to thy ears? Or the sky to offer its blue carriage? Or the ocean to wash upon the shores of Heaven?"

There are words I do not know that seek to find their way across my lips to God's ears. I have no sense of their origin, yet they rise in my mind with conviction and look for expression. From a language long forgotten, with praise that has never found its outlet, these words align themselves, waiting to be heard. Glowing and patient for their turn, composing their meaning as they rise from somewhere deep within me, these words seek their greatest expression from the smallest of origins. *How dramatic their appearances while falling short of the fullness that they seek?* My heart swells with joy in moments where I know firsthand the knowledge that lies within the great books of time. These fleeting glimpses, penetrating and all-consuming, lie before me. I can sense an opening to the fullness of Creation, a hint of meaning reaching out and grasping for the hand of my Creator. So few are my moments of the sublime where all is well, at peace and right. "Lord, what is there that keeps us apart while bound so completely. My desire is only to know thee, and thy will is to be known. Why then is it not so? Painfully infrequent, so short are these moments together that reassure and comfort while increasing my need for thy presence all the more. Stay with me, accompany me as I seek greater worthiness that I may earn thy recognition, respect, and constant presence."

***

Over the last century there has been a steady increase in the incidence of cancer in the United States. Despite the vast amounts of money directed toward gaining a better understanding and a cure, it continues its deadly reign, ravaging at every level of society. Most people have a friend or family member who has been touched by this devastating disease.

My brother Fred began to experience some health issues in 1977; it was soon determined that he had a brain tumor. His illness was a shock to all of us. Strong, smart, and active, he loved his wife and two young children...he loved his life. This disease was in sharp contrast to his nature; it just did not make sense. We denied that he could be overcome by cancer, and that denial fueled our optimism that he could win his fight with the dreaded disease. Never one to complain, he went on living his life as the disease progressed; however, after months of treatment, surgery, and medications, it appeared Fred was losing the battle we all had prayed he would win.

At one point during this time, he was to go fishing with some good friends from the old days in the projects. All these years later they had remained close. Fred was to meet them at their home in Elizaville, New York. I drove him into New York City to catch the train for his trip. Along the way we talked very little about what might happen as his disease progressed. His outlook was typically positive, but he did become solemn when he talked about a recurring dream he had been having. The dream troubled him. He would find himself out in the ocean, submerged below the surface. His arm was able to break through and extend above the waves, but he could not bring himself above water. He could feel the air, and the sun warmed his arm, but he could not rise. He said the dream always ended the same: without ever resolving the situation, he would awaken. As he shared his dream, he sought no counsel or consolation. Fred was a fatalist; ever optimistic, reluctant to give in and willing to fight, he still understood and accepted the reality of the situation. He said, "We'll just have to see what happens." That fishing trip provided him with a nice break from his routine and treatment; he was able, for one last time, to connect with his friends and enjoy the outdoors.

Watching those you love suffer, slowly losing their vibrancy, is one of the greatest torments in life. Despite my new-found understanding of life through meditation, I still struggled with the presence of suffering in our world. Karmic, fateful, and judicious expressions, wise in their logic, offered little comfort for what I was witnessing. Fred was my big brother. He was my protector, my teacher, and my companion with whom all things large and small could be shared – and I had no way to help change the course of his affliction.

Having survived as a Marine in Vietnam, one would have thought the worst fight he would have to endure in this life was already behind him; yet life acquainted him with this further indignity – and this time it was a struggle that could not be overcome by sheer willpower. A certain, unfair, and indiscriminate determinism had beset his world with a resolute indifference. Life had failed to interpret, on the scales of justice, the value inherent to the continuation of his life. He had not been afforded counsel to represent his character, his purpose, or his most basic desire: to live. As the months dragged on, Fred's situation worsened; seizures, nausea, fatigue, and an unquestionable awareness of his fate plagued him.

On the last night that I spoke with Fred, we were hanging out in his living room watching some senseless horror movie. We talked periodically into the night as the rest of his family lay sleeping. I could see he was not feeling well. I felt that he should get some sleep and, thus, decided to end our visit early. I shook his hand, in the grasp of the time, and told him I would see him "tomorrow." He looked at me and said only one thing: "Thanks." It was as if he was saying a goodbye. This sole word is part of my lasting final memory of a great brother, a friend, and a decent human being. The next morning Fred was taken by ambulance to the hospital. When I reached his bedside he was already in a coma, unresponsive, without the joy or the vitality that was my brother. A respirator beside his bed had taken on the task of his breathing; it carried out its work with an efficient but disquieting rhythm, allowing his body to endure. Whenever I had the chance to go to the hospital, I would stand beside his bed speaking to him about everything (and nothing in particular) as the respirator pulsed and the monitors beeped; I hoped my words would penetrate his condition and register inside of him. He remained in that coma for several weeks, until August 9, 1977, when he passed from this life. Fred not only left behind a family, but he left a hole in the hearts of everyone who knew him. He was just 29 years old.

Fred's cancer and resulting death made me wonder if Vietnam had still been haunting his body, the same way it haunted his mind. The side effects of Agent Orange (an herbicide used extensively in Vietnam, to which our soldiers had been exposed during the war) were just now beginning to come to light. A long list of cancers and serious health issues, including birth defects in veterans' children, were now documented and left for us to consider.

Struggling with his departure, all words of consolation fell short of explanation. This free-spirited and fun-loving husband, father, son, and brother had moved on to that which awaits all of us...but he was taken from us in a heartless way, and his departure was far too premature. I was angry with death, with the reaper who harvested souls. I understood the way of things – the decrees of nature and the allotment of days – but...if only we could choose the time and place.

As the priest created a purifying veil of frankincense above the coffin, a fragrant cloud rose eerily around the church pew. As it mixed with the prevailing smell of flowers, my senses were consumed. I sat half aware, distracted in grief as the crowded, sacred ceremony continued. Already well under way, the formal, mystical goodbye of our Catholic faith was punctuated by offerings in a long-forgotten Latin language, familiar in sound but not in meaning. Officiated by a representative of our Creator here on Earth and in keeping with the ages-old ritual, spiritual declarations and a sacred script of prayers were recited by those in attendance. This was the formal spiritual preparation for whatever awaits us all beyond this life; the sacramental connection between the departed and those who lived on, breaching the unseen gap between the living, the dead, and our Creator. Each of those present had been touched by my brother's life, and each held their own sense of grief as they considered thoughts of life without him.

The old church organ was brought to life, bellowing deep, melancholy sounds. It was accompanied by a lone soloist skilled at creating a reverent, somber air. Her voice rang out in full command of the hallowed church acoustics, providing some comforting and familiar – while, at the same time, depressing – melodies and conjuring up memories akin to such assemblies attended in the past. All of the melodies were befitting the circumstances, of course; yet I wondered if Fred would have preferred something more irreverent, bold, and raucous (such was his nature) to try to change the air of sadness surrounding his final farewell. Perhaps The Doors or The Rolling Stones? He had a great love of music. I can still hear the Beach Boys' albums playing on our old record player during summers in the early 1960's, a time of innocence and stepping into the bigger world around us. Or maybe, in lieu of music, Fred would have preferred some maddening rants from his favorite Irish author and novelist, James Joyce. He was captivated by the author's complex writing of *Ulysses* and *Finnegan's Wake*. At one point he even traveled to Dublin University, to study where Joyce himself once studied. I believe he sought to connect with Joyce's old environs in hopes of gaining a greater insight into the man with whom he was so fascinated.

These wanderings of my mind at such a time were absurd, perhaps inexcusable; but they were earnest reflections as Fred's life was still fresh in my awareness, his death not yet real. The religious images that dominated my vision helped me regain a contemporary focus. Light sought its way into the house of worship through the colorful stained glass windows. The altar – marble, gold, and statuary – somehow brought strength and reassurance to our final gathering. Beyond some quiet sobbing, an occasional cough, or some restless shuffling, hardly a sound disturbed the course of the solemn ceremony. The priest moved at a dignified pace as he passed before me in his heavily-starched vestments. The young altar boys assisting him were innocent, much too young to fully appreciate the serious nature of the ritual in which they now took part; they reminded me of the times that my brother and I once served the same function.

My mind, once again straying from the service, sought out moments we shared together. One of the many adventures from our youth came to mind. We were maybe 15 and 16, respectively, and had convinced our parents to let us go alone on a camping trip to our cabin in Rowlands, Pennsylvania. We were not very skilled at camping and, as a result, had carried with us more than we needed. After arriving at a nearby town on a

Greyhound bus, we walked several miles to our destination. We decided to camp along the Lackawaxen River, in the same area where our family had nearly drowned years ago. It was dark by the time we crossed the river to set up our campsite. We placed our tent at what we thought was the base of a small hill and, exhausted from our long trek, were soon asleep. Deep into our sleep we were abruptly startled to wakefulness in the unfamiliar darkness. It seemed that an earthquake was upon us, and we swore we also heard the scream of a tornado. Terrified, we scrambled out of the tent – not knowing what was happening or what to do – only to be blinded by the lights of a roaring freight train. In our haste to set up camp in the darkness, we had done so beside a railroad track. The vibration of the train and the wind produced by its massive passing were frightening. It truly scared the shit out of us. After some time, we were able to laugh about the incident. Fred and I had been adventurous in our youth and together enjoyed the simple entertainment of life. It was sad his body no longer lived while his spirit continued its journey.

I was at peace with Fred's passing, though uncomfortable as my life and that of his loved ones went on without him. I thought about his life and the things he loved: music, literature, fighting for veterans' rights, and partying. The expression of my pain was more about me than anything else – my loss by separation, devoid of a greater understanding of life. So selfish is grief with its gloomy embrace displacing the joy of the lives we once knew. So natural is grief in the way it rises up from within us, unable to find expression on the faces of some while all too clear on others. *Does the world outside of man mourn his loss?*

When the ceremony reached its conclusion, we rose respectfully as his consecrated body was readied for its trip to his final resting place for its relative eternity. Drawn together behind him, we slowly accompanied his earthly being toward the light of the opened doors at the far end of the church. Each slow and painful step ushered us past those also connected to him in this life; we offered each other expressions of support. At last clearing the confines of the church, we broke into the reassuring sunshine of the early August day. When we arrived at his mausoleum, I was struck by the fact that, as kids, we would traverse this centuries-old, sprawling cemetery in search of rabbits and pheasants. Shared with the likes of the Vanderbilt's, it was a beautiful resting place, crowded with ancient oaks that stood guard while shading the consecrated ground. Having completed his role here on Earth, Fred had been ushered from the stage of life and on to other, greater performances.

Relapsing at times with the realization that he was no longer with us, we shared endless stories about Fred – from the ordinary to the insane – with friends and family at a reception after the ceremony. His essence would endure and grow along with us in our collective memory. My brother's life had been brilliant and meaningful – a complete work of art.

I still oftentimes speak to Fred as though he were right in front of me. His image, somewhat faded, endures in my mind and allows for spontaneous reunions where he greets me with his characteristic smile, amidst the quietest or busiest of times. He visits my dreams, reliving moments we shared in our time together in this life. I share the disappointments, accomplishments, sadness, and joy that I continue to experience without him; knowing how he would react, I can clearly hear his voice in support or condemnation.

***

There plays in this world a collective symphony of sadness, joy, and wonder. As the unapprised tears of man fall, they sound for him a note of discord within the masterpiece that is Creation. A greater mind sees no less pain in life but only sees it for what it is: the notes that comprise the chords of Creation are resolute, pure, and eternal.

Pain and sadness, in their many forms, are inescapable and difficult to reconcile while part of a compassionate universe. Mind, body, and spirit, none are immune to the discomforts of life. We are of the human condition, subject to the contrasts of time but singularly able to know the source of our existence.

Delicate flowers amongst the extreme density of inanimate and living things, we are the pinnacle of Creation, prized by the Creator. Blessed, but unaware of our value, we are paupers dressed in the vision of humanity, blind to the riches we possess. We are never far from the Creator for we move and exist as one.

As we each evolve and our individual ego (the mind's function of our sense of self) rises to its eventual universal status, the perceived inequities of life are understood in a different light. The disposition of life is the purview of He who has created that in which we dwell. Ours is but to evolve, to grow in understanding, to search and appreciate this mystery in which we live. Uncomplicated, easy, and joyous - yet at the same time, how easily misunderstood, difficult, and terrible – is Creation. It can only be seen as a gift; we can only be thankful we *are*.

The stage is set. We are both players and spectators in the play of Creation, unknowingly watching ourselves perform. We are each supremely important in this play, while not one of us is anyone special...there are always understudies ready to take our place center stage as we retire.

***

In 1978, in the midst of the impending Iranian revolution, a small group of TM instructors were organized with the intention of going to Tehran. Their mission was simple: to congregate in the capital and meditate in an attempt to counter the negative influence being generated by the Ayatollahs. Ideally, they would be able to introduce TM into that country. Intrigued by the potential of this undertaking, I was compelled to join the group. I was convinced that the influence each of us generates into our environment has a profound effect on those with whom we interact. Without a word, we contribute to our sphere of activity; thus, a unified positive influence amidst the darkest of malevolent forces could have a weakening effect (if ever so little) on the darkness. Our contribution would not be with the spoken word but with the unspoken peace we would generate. Like a single candle in a dark room, our collective energy would help dispel the gloom of those saddened, unfulfilled, and discouraged by life. Our methods may have seemed unconventional and unheard of – insane, even – but I believed it was worth a try. It would be an experiment, esoteric in nature, making it all the more alluring by the danger inherent to the challenge. In retrospect, our undertaking was akin to metaphysical espionage (if such a thing does, in fact, exist).

I joined the group with my friend Randy. We were instructed to keep our travel plans and our intentions once we arrived to ourselves. Iran was a revolutionary Islamic state. We were sure we would never have been granted a visa if they knew what we had planned; if discovered once there, we would surely be jailed. It had never really occurred to me how dangerous it would be to embark on this journey. There was a lot of turmoil in Iran at the time; it was quickly becoming a precarious, unpredictable place. Undaunted by the circumstances and believing we could make a difference, we proceeded.

We went to the Iranian Embassy in New York City to obtain our visas as a group of about 50 "cultural exchange students." I felt very uncomfortable throughout the short time we were in the embassy. Everyone I dealt with seemed suspicious, challenging each of us with questions regarding our desire to go to Tehran. Having known the scrutiny we would encounter, we were well prepared, armed with responses that would not send up any red flags. We were informed of the strict prohibitions regarding a visit to Iran and told what vaccinations would be necessary before entering the country.

By this time I had been an instructor of TM for about three years. I had witnessed the powerful effects of meditation on both a personal and social level. It had drawn me out of habitual drug use and brought the wonders of Creation to the forefront of my consciousness. If there was a chance, however remote, that we could make a difference in Tehran, I was willing to travel to that troubled place. We received our shots, our visas were approved, and we awaited our departure. Shortly before we were to leave, we received word that the project had been called off; we would not be going to Tehran. Never quite sure what prompted the change of plans and disappointed by the cancellation of the trip, I have often since wondered what it might have been like had the trip materialized. In February of 1979, three short months after our clandestine trip was canceled, the Shah of Iran was overthrown and fled to Europe. No more than nine months later, on November 4, 1979, the volatile situation culminated with the U.S. Embassy in Tehran under siege and ultimately taken over by radical Islamic students. A total of 52 Americans, diplomats and citizens, were held hostage and tormented over a period of 444 days of captivity; they were finally released on January 20, 1981. I was taken aback by what was happening and began to experience a rash of *what ifs* had our travel plans come to fruition. That was my last (albeit unfulfilled) clandestine adventure to promote world peace.

***

Having devoted several years to the TM organization, contributing what I could to the cause of world peace, I felt myself being drawn away from my spiritual pursuits and the world of meditation. My time as a TM teacher and my studies at MIU had brought me valuable spiritual insights that would always be my confidantes, but I found it was time to devote my energies elsewhere. My father provided the impetus I was seeking to focus on my nagging creative impulses.

Most inventors, philosophers, and great thinkers tend to be seen as eccentric, unstable, or out of touch with reality until they and their ideas are understood. *Who are we to qualify their behavior until that time? At what point does grandiose thought actually become insanity?* My father shared the qualities of the great thinkers and seemed to draw unto himself those of like mind, those who believed that all things were possible and thought differently from the average person. So it was that this thinking brought him into association with an inventor and "the invention" – his latest and greatest recipient of the title "best idea ever."

138

"What a great idea! Listen to this." As my father shared, in the most secretive of tones, his encounter with this particular inventor, I must admit that I was spellbound. I drew my chair closer to him and was quickly caught up in the momentum that he had generated regarding this, his latest endeavor. In short order he had already enlisted the aid of three other trusted friends to share in the joy of this invention and participate in its production. It all seemed to make sense, and it would change the world: a system that would harness the power of hydraulic pressure to produce inexpensive energy. The proposed configuration of batteries and hydraulic motors and pumps would be capable of creating a tremendous amount of energy for a variety of essential uses, for both private and commercial consumption.

Our team of six was eager to share in the excitement that could ensue if this dream was, in fact, realized. We were all hopeful, enthusiastic, supportive, and protective of the inventor's brainchild. So there we were, sitting around the table: me, my father, the inventor, a truck driver, an attorney, and a ship's captain. Save for myself, all recovering alcoholics. Cigarette smoke rose and mingled above the table at our weekly meetings, creating a cloud upon which we all rode; it seemed to capture the ephemeral nature of our inventive minds. With my father at the helm of our seaworthy adventure, we set out to change the world. It was clear from the beginning that our voyage would be on choppy seas.

Our home served as the headquarters of the newly-formed corporation "Creative Energy Technologies." At each of our weekly meetings, the corporate table in our kitchen hosted loud discussions on how to proceed; it was covered with piles of paper, sketches, trade journals, ashtrays, bagels, and coffee. Each member of our group was strong-willed, a good quality in business but one that made difficult decisions even harder. In spite of my father's short fuse, sudden violent outbursts (already known to, and expected by, all present), and impatient nature, we moved forward, ever mindful of how quickly the whole idea could fall apart – we could not let that happen.

With the exception of the inventor, Jack, I had known all of the members of our group for some time, and I trusted them. I couldn't say for sure what it was about Jack, but from the moment I first met him I had a poor instinctive reading. Something about him seemed off when I made direct eye contact with him. He was awkward and lacked openness, despite his congenial ways; he bordered on paranoid. I passed it off as nervousness as he was trying to develop the trust necessary to hand his invention over to strangers. After all, I wasn't quite sure that Jack was completely comfortable with who he was dealing with either (several of our crew had pasts that, although never confirmed, involved perilous altercations).

One thing that should have given us all pause for concern from the very beginning was that we didn't have a working model. Jack said he had previously constructed the machine, and that it had successfully performed to his expectations. He claimed to have dismantled the machine (for reasons in line with his paranoia) but kept the schematics of the invention for later patenting. This is where we came in: we were being entrusted to bring his invention through the patenting process and then negotiate its licensing. So, we were working on trust and schematics to realize and develop an invention that, if successful, would significantly change all of our lives.

Everything that happened at our meetings was held in the strictest of confidence. Working amid a mutual paranoia of the corporate world, our crew discussed the first orders of business: to enlist the aid of a patent attorney and to obtain a patent in the name of the corporation. We found that filing a patent was a costly process that would take much longer than our enthusiasm-fueled projections had accounted for, but we were all convinced the endeavor was worth the time. There was (and could be) no doubt that this was the next big thing in the world of energy production.

Still, Jack was reluctant to actually display the invention until the patenting process was complete; his reluctance bolstered my lingering suspicions. I tried to convince myself he was simply being overly cautious; after all, it was inconceivable that he would have led us through this process without a legitimate product. We all had too much invested to see it any differently. We had to keep focused on how fortunate we were to be a part of bringing this invention to market. We allowed our contagious excitement to overwhelm any skepticism that surfaced along the way.

We continued to work with our patent attorney to ensure we submitted a patent application that was rock solid, able to withstand any claims of infringement by owners of existing patents. It was difficult and exacting work, but it was necessary because of the broad claims in the language of those existing patents. Time dragged on until we finally filed our application. We waited patiently for the process to advance through the U.S. Patent Office. At one point we hit a snag: they were going to deny our application because of our claim that the invention could continually power itself. It would be a claim of perpetual motion, which is something that is not patentable. We straightened out the wording of the patent, and the process of review began once again. While we anxiously awaited the patent to be issued, we began to focus on what we would do once the invention was officially registered. Each member of our group had his own commitments; but, while we were all engaged in different things, our involvement with the invention preoccupied our minds for a good portion of our working days. Having been diagnosed with vertigo and, thus, now retired from construction, my father spent his days surrounded by mounds of books and papers related to our patent, studying how it could be applied in different industries. I would say he was genuinely obsessed with the whole process.

By this point we had already invested a lot of time, effort, and money into the invention. We now needed Jack to construct a much-coveted model. We told him to provide us with a list of the parts that would be necessary to begin assembly and sought (to no avail) a timetable for its completion. Though we offered our assistance in construction, Jack preferred to work alone; and so we waited. During this time we contacted an executive from

Rockwell International to meet with us in a confidential discussion of our impending patent and its licensing. We were all very excited as this was a big deal; we had finally reached the point we had been working toward for so long.

We were getting down to the wire. Our meeting with Rockwell was fast approaching, and Jack was not present for an important Saturday meeting to give an update on his progress. We called his home over and over, but we could not reach him. My father repeatedly shouted, "Where the fuck is Jack?" When we finally reached him the following day, he offered the plausible excuse that he had been working on the motor in an undisclosed location (for security reasons) and had completely lost track of time as he was so intent to finish his work. He assured us that he would be ready to demonstrate the motor. We were all annoyed with him but relieved to hear that things were progressing – they had to be, we were all depending on this. We were unaware of it then, but we were about to witness the death spiral for that which we had worked so hard to achieve.

I believe it was Shakespeare who once suggested that each of us in our lifetime will play the role of a fool; and so it was that these five ordinary men, who had spent countless hours developing a patent to bring to market an invention that could have changed the lives of man, sat facing each other in disbelief. Herb, the member of our group who was closest to Jack, shared the news: "Jack is drunk incoherent. He is out of his fucking mind. I hunted that fucker down." Herb was crazy with anger as he continued: "There is no fucking invention. Just a pile of shit parts, sketches, schematics, and empty beer cans. Everything is unassembled, lying in his garage in Brooklyn."

We later discovered that Jack had been mentally ill for some time. As it turned out, he had successfully been able to pass off his peculiar nature as the eccentricity of an inventor. As angry as I was toward Jack, I was fearful for his safety. I could see the frightful rage welling up in my father's eyes as Herb gave us the shocking news. It was a look I had witnessed many times over the years – a look I knew would not bode well for the target of his anger once it was unleashed. My father and Herb shared a strong bond: they each had the air of an unspoken past that carried the specific understanding that each was capable of imposing great harm when pushed to his limit. I had never seen my father so upset by something. If I was to hear that some harm had befallen Jack following this news, it would not have been a surprise.

We shared the look of someone who had just lost his life savings at a gambling table, having bet everything on one throw of the dice only to lose it all. We had invested our trust, support, and encouragement only to be subjected to the worst sort of betrayal. Shattered, angry, and in utter disbelief, we all wondered how this could have happened. *How could all five of us have been so totally misled by this one man?* Our collective vision had just been blinded. It was a death of sorts – the death of something we were just giving birth to – and we mourned its premature departure. The hopes we had shared for humanity and ourselves were now dashed. After some inquiries to further satisfy our disbelief, we confirmed that Jack, our supposed key to a better life, was truly (as my father summed it all up) "a fucking nut."

On leaving our corporate table for the last time, we were all tired, devastated, and embarrassed to have been so genuinely betrayed. In one last attempt to make some sense of what remained of the invention, Herb tried unsuccessfully to construct it on his own. In a gesture of disgust and anger, he dumped everything related to Jack and the invention off a pier in New Jersey. It had all been a bad dream.

We dismantled our corporate group of entrepreneurs and would-be corporate titans and returned to our separate lives – disillusioned, angry, and maybe a bit wiser. Several months later my father received a letter from the patent attorney. It contained the news we had all looked forward to for so long: our patent had been issued. It was a peculiar feeling to know we had patented something we had never seen, never touched; yet here it was in my father's hand – a glaring example of trust gone wrong, a twisted bit of fate. Embarrassing in its timing, the patent was a further torment for all involved. Reopening our wound, United States Patent #4663937 served as a grand display of our naïveté, the permanent record of an unsuccessful venture while embracing the potential genius of a madman.

Jack died of cancer some short time after our invention fiasco. I was never really interested in finding out exactly how he died; and, sorry to say, I was not all that saddened by the news. Thus ended another chapter in my father's book of creative endeavors; although a big blow, he would never lose his passion for following the wild dreams of his imagination. He had always said that the best thing you could do if you were thrown from a horse was to get right back on; and so he did. Undeterred by the failure of Creative Energy Technologies, he would soon be off in pursuit of his next "best idea ever" with an ever-present entrepreneurial optimism.

Staten Island, New York
Late 1960's

It was just before dinner on a typically hectic Friday night in the spring of 1966. Everyone was gathered around the kitchen table waiting to eat. Good Catholics that we were, Friday night always meant we would be having fish. A sudden knock at the door brought my attention to the familiar, and obviously drunk, face of Joe K. In a family of alcoholics, we could all sense that the visit was not going to go well: the stage was set for a confrontation on the home front. My father was scheduled to take Joe to an AA meeting, but was currently on the phone with another drunken charge. He acknowledged Joe's arrival with a nod as we brought him into the kitchen. In the short time before my father hung up the phone, Joe had made his way around our kitchen, inspecting the fish cooking on the stove and making comments about everything; all the while, he was under my father's vigilant eye and clearly considered out of order. Getting loud and disruptive, Joe got up in my brother Fred's face, challenging him about how tough he was. Suddenly, my father moved to Joe's side and landed a lightning quick punch to his face that carried with it the awful, crunching sound of the cartilage in his nose. Joe fell to the floor and cracked his head on the big cast-iron radiator in the corner of the room on his way down. In just some few moments our kitchen had become a madhouse: there was blood everywhere; our dog was barking wildly; and my mother was yelling for them to stop as she tried her best to save the dinner cooking on the stove. Joe was on the floor, bleeding heavily, while Fred and I tried our best to control our father, the now madman, from kicking him in the head. Each of us latched onto one of his arms in an attempt to steer him away from the man who had disrespected his home and family. It was my first real view of the rage that dwelled inside my father. There had been other instances where I had seen him go crazy, but never anything like this. I likened the incident to seeing a wild animal attacking its prey. His eyes – the windows to the soul – especially scared me; in an instant they had become dark red and evil. Fred and I managed to separate the men long enough to drag Joe out of the kitchen and then out of the house. All the while, my mother kept trying to quell the tempest that fell upon her kitchen as she had been preparing dinner. Once revived, Joe wanted to come back in to apologize; but Fred and I discouraged him, sending him on his drunken way – bleeding, disheveled, and (in our eyes) lucky to be alive. We returned to the kitchen to right the overturned chairs and straighten out our beloved table. We could see our father had returned from whatever demonic place he had just visited. He questioned, to no one in particular, "Is that son of a bitch gone?" We assured him that Joe was on his way and would not be coming back.

In the typical alcoholic-family fashion, we quickly tried to come back from the traumatic event by acting like nothing out of the ordinary had happened. We put on our best faces in the aftermath, trying to return things to a state of normalcy. It was as though by acting like everything was okay, it would be so; of course, it was not. My younger brother, Jimmy, looked on in disbelief as my mother tended to the now-overcooked fish. My sister, Annie, tried to infuse some humor into the situation by commenting about how I had looked like a rag doll being tossed around while holding onto my father's arm. My father had to be embarrassed, taken aback by displaying such violent behavior in front of his family. As we all sat around the table for dinner, he spoke some few words about the "goddamn asshole...the dopey bastard" who had shown up drunk, but spoke no words of comfort for his family. Eating, of course, was difficult as we all found it hard to swallow after such an upsetting scene.

My father's demeanor carried the effects of his adrenaline surge well into dinner and (to some lesser extent) up until the time he left for his AA meeting. As he left, there was a quiet, unified sigh of relief. He would be gone, as usual, for a few hours. Sorry to say, we all felt better when he left the house because there was a temporary reprieve from his unpredictability. It is sad, but true that there were times when I hoped he would not come home. I wondered why he couldn't be more like other fathers. What a terrible way to feel about my own flesh and blood – a child should not feel this way about his father. I had been taught to honor my father and mother; it was a basic tenant of my religious foundation. *What anger was there inside of me that could bring such thoughts to abide within my mind? Was it some abrogation of my duties as a son to hold him in such disdain? Or were my feelings justified, supported by a host of transgressions, large and small, both personal to me and general in nature? Was I short of forgiveness or just so tired of observing the lapses of normal conduct?*

The oppressive weather of addiction brought with it an emotional humidity that hung heavily around our family. The climate of uncertainty could not be clearly forecasted; it was precipitated by unknown elements. Life was a matter of degrees of changing patterns. Pressure of one form or another could inevitably bring about the winds of change. Fronts would unavoidably collide, contesting each other's energy until one prevailed or both dissipated. The clinging to hope for fair weather contrasted with the withering of sunshine and the contraction of goodwill that played out amongst our weathered

146

spirits. Instinctively avoiding storms visible on the horizon and moving away from threats to quieter, safer quarters, I desperately sought shelter from the fear of witnessing his explosive behavior, the humiliation of our family, and perhaps the realization that I might one day find within myself the very things I hated about him.

***

Over the years I often wondered how my father had managed to survive as long as he had. One morning, as I sat with him at the kitchen table to remove some stitches from his hand, I asked how many stitches he had thus far throughout his life. He said he couldn't remember, just that most were sewn into his head and face. The number of fingers he had broken in fights was also lost in the haze of the past. *What had it been that created the foundation for the aggression and violence that were so much a part of his life?* I failed to see anything in particular from what I knew of his childhood that would account for his volatile personality. I kept returning to the years he spent fighting in the Pacific during World War II as the probable source of his aggression; not that the war could fully explain all of his negative attributes, but it had certainly contributed to many of them.

Outside of AA, my father was uncomfortable in social situations; attendance at weddings, birthdays, and picnics was out of the question. He did not seem to take joy in any activities or pastimes. Many of those who found solace within the walls of AA exhibited similar strained social traits; after all, alcohol had once proven to be the remedy for overcoming such discomfort and reducing their inhibitions. Despite his social constraints my father had a command, an ease at communicating in a powerful and effective manner, when speaking to alcoholics in any venue. Having reestablished some sense of normalcy after his own life insolvent of body, mind, and spirit, he had words of hope to share with those similarly infected. His vocabulary was one cultured from the painful experience of the low points of addiction. Simply put, he spoke the language of the alcoholic.

Staten Island, New York
Late 1970's

The unfortunate dissolution of Creative Energy Technologies had left my father bitter for a time, but it had not dampened his creative spirit. As the old saying goes, "the hair of the dog" was the medicine he needed to break free from the grasp of failure. He would often recount the well-worn story, told by entrepreneurial types, of the number of times Edison failed before finally perfecting his light bulb. So, with another bad light bulb behind us, we devoted ourselves to our next creative endeavor.

After a short stay in the hospital for a minor health issue, my father became very aware of the lack of a patient's desire to eat hospital food. He attributed it, in part, to the lack of olfactory stimulation in the hospital rooms: patients couldn't smell the food being cooked. He decided that creating a means to stimulate their desire to eat could be achieved by introducing familiar food fragrances into hospital rooms before meals. My father felt those who had no appetite, specifically those confined to a hospital bed, would benefit from the use of a product that could imitate the smell of food preparation ordinarily missing in sterile environments. It was simple logic as far as he was concerned: "Who is there that is not stimulated by the smell of brewing coffee or the aroma of fresh-baked bread?"

It was with this premise in mind that "Koala Naturals" came into being. Our mission was to create food fragrances and to devise a way to disburse them into hospital rooms. Relying on the use of essential oils and propellants, careful to avoid the use of fluorocarbons, we entered the world of sensory stimulation. In 1979 we were years ahead of the aroma therapy industry. As spokesman, armed only with enthusiasm, I proposed our idea to one of the world's largest perfume houses, International Flavors and Fragrances. They were receptive, and so we began our marketing efforts in earnest.

Our company name had been born out of one of the first products we developed, an aerosol made from eucalyptus oil. That product was followed soon after by a spearmint and peppermint product. After several months of working together, the perfume house allowed me to propose the development of new experimental food fragrances to their chemists. I was like a kid in a candy store when they let my imagination run wild; it was a blast. Over the course of several years, we developed nearly 35 different products, many of which proved unsuccessful as they did not translate well into an aerosol distribution. We did, however, achieve our goal with the fragrances for baked bread, coffee, and roast pork.

We had given the idea our best effort and had many close calls with success, but we always seemed to be just shy of where we needed to be. Quantas Airlines had expressed interest in our eucalyptus spray as a promotion on their flights, the Boy Scouts were using our products for fundraisers, and a large food chain was interested in placing our products on their shelves, but we were unsuccessful in what had motivated us originally: bringing the food fragrances into a hospital setting. The studies that would be required to eliminate liability (for a host of reasons, including allergies) made it impossible to gain acceptance for our products. The most difficult thing for both my father and I was knowing when it was time to quit; once the desire to realize our goal had taken hold, our vision had become clouded by an entrepreneurial fog. Mounting debt and the distasteful realization of futility provided the impetus we needed; and so we slowly concluded our final chapter in this, the latest business venture expected to change our lives.

***

A short time after the dissolution of Koala Naturals, I received a call from my sister, Annie. She told me our father was drunk. It's hard to describe the emotions that such news generated. I immediately got a knot in my stomach, followed by a sense of hyperawareness. I asked, "Where is he now?" Annie said she didn't know, but there were two other problems I needed to be aware of: he was driving, and he was carrying a gun.

Our father had been free from alcohol for 22 years; yet the experience of how it affected him, and the knowledge of what he was capable of when under the influence, were fresh in our minds. He had overcome his demons and held them at bay for so long; and he had helped scores of people to do the same. The why and the how of the situation were not immediately clear and only secondary to our desire to find him. He was, as the psychologists would say, "a clear danger to himself and to others." We had no idea where he was or where he might be going. What troubled me more than anything was the fact that he was in possession of a gun. I could only wonder if there was someone with whom he had a vendetta (recent in nature or from his past, whether real or imagined); regardless, it was imperative we locate him.

I joined Annie, my wife, and my mother at the house. We called everyone he knew in hopes that someone might have had some contact with him, but our efforts were to no avail. We were all frantic, trying our best to be reassuring to one another despite knowing precisely how serious the situation was. I thought I might encounter him around one of the local bars or liquor stores, and so I decided to drive through the neighborhood. There was no telling what he was up to or where he was going. It reminded me of a time some years earlier when he had been hospitalized because of a relapse of the malaria he had acquired in the jungles of New Guinea during World War II. While delirious from fever, he had decided that he needed to get away from the hospital and complete his recovery at home. He proceeded to make his escape in a hospital gown and slippers. Carrying a handful of change, as he had no pockets in the gown, he somehow managed to travel through Manhattan and all the way home to Staten Island via the ferry. He could be very single-minded when he chose to do something.

After a few hours of anxious searching, we received a call from a family friend in New Jersey who said that my father was at his house. He had shown up mysteriously, and his behavior was making our friends more than a little nervous. We asked them to try to keep him there until we could retrieve him, but they called again some minutes later to tell us he was back on the road, driving home to Staten Island (on two flat front tires no less). To get home, he would have to cross the Outer Bridge that connected Staten Island to New Jersey; that meant he would have to stop at the toll booth. We felt he would certainly be arrested by the police who were always present at the bridge: he was driving drunk; the car had two flat tires; and he had a gun. Just being in possession of a handgun in New Jersey or New York was, in itself, a very serious offense. We prayed that, at the very least, he would keep his temper in check, and there would not be a confrontation.

Time passed slowly as we awaited contact from either my father or the authorities. Several hours later, his tires shredded from the rims, he somehow arrived home in one piece. How he managed to drive the car, and why he wasn't stopped by the police as he drove across the bridge and around Staten Island, remained a mystery. My father's good friend Herb, who had joined us in our search a few hours earlier, first spotted him parking the car. Herb was able to relieve him of his pistol before escorting him into the house. I was sitting in the kitchen when he came through the front door and was greeted by my mother. When our eyes met he simply said, as if a fight were imminent, "Here's trouble." Throughout my youth we were always at odds with one another and knew to give each other some distance during arguments because of the explosive natures of our personalities. However, given his state of mind, it was surprising that I would be seen by him as a threat. Assured by my mother that I was not looking for an altercation, he removed his coat and awkwardly sat down at the kitchen table, somewhat subdued. Like an animal released from a cage after being held captive for a long time, he seemed reluctant to trust his environment and those in it.

Here before me was a man who knew all the dangers of alcohol and all the reasons why he shouldn't drink. As I looked at

151

him, I couldn't help but feel confused, angry, and sorry for him all at the same time. He was a man with a lot of pride; once he returned from whatever place he currently dwelled, the understanding that he had fallen prey to his old demons would surely assault his self-image in a most hurtful way. My mother (God bless her) dealt with him as best she could. In an attempt to reestablish some normalcy, she asked if he was hungry, what had happened, and if he was okay. Being humbled was not something my father was good at. In the months to come, he would have to endure the humiliation of having failed himself and, in his eyes, others. It would truly be one of his greatest challenges to face those who had seen him as rock steady; those who looked to him for guidance, support, and inspiration; those who he had helped to free themselves from the bonds of alcohol; those who had listened to his many persuasive, forceful, and charismatic declarations on the need to maintain sobriety. His words had been grounded in experience – and they were real, meaningful, and authentic – but they were now tarnished by his fall from grace.

Herb took me aside to give me the recovered gun. I unloaded it and stashed it in my coat before returning to the table. By now Charlie S. had also joined us; and together with my mother, my wife, my sister, and Herb, we sat talking with my father for several awkward hours until he finally agreed to go to bed. During our conversations we gained little information about what prompted him to begin drinking that night. We felt he might share the reason with us in the days to come, if he even remembered. We were content for now to have him home, off the streets and unarmed; for that, we were thankful.

My father returned to reality after a few days. His 22 years of continued sobriety was now a thing of the past. He would have to start over from day one, dealing with life one day at a time. Humiliated or not, it was what he had to do; and so began his return to the rooms of AA. The smoky rented halls and classrooms in the church basements with which he was once so comfortable now became difficult to navigate. I could see the starch taken out of him. I could read the loss of self-confidence on his countenance. He had given in to the self-destructive nature that perpetually lies in wait beneath the surface of a recovering alcoholic. For him, there could be no self-exile; he could only accept what happened and face that reality. Over time, through his determined nature and with support of those around him, he was nurtured back to his former self. Scarred, but stronger and wiser because of his slip from sobriety, he went back to work doing what he did best: helping other people get and stay sober. We could never say for sure what had prompted his fall from grace, but we speculated it could have been a stroke (the result of all the head injuries he had experienced over the years).

Regardless of what had caused his slip, I had no doubt that my father would be hard on himself for the transgression. Hopefully he would show himself the same understanding he had managed to show his charges over the years when they experienced challenges with their sobriety.

***

We had grown up in a different time – a time where discipline was expected, important, and (acceptably) enforceable by corporal punishment. We all understood this and what it meant if you stepped out of line. For us, it meant that major transgressions would result in the application of my father's belt to our backsides. Never used to excess in our home, it was a deterrent passed down from previous generations; and, unpleasant as it might have been, it was not an uncommon form of household discipline. I once came across a letter that my older brother, Fred, had written to our father after our mother had sent him to bed as punishment for an unusually rowdy incident.

Dad, I am sorry for the trouble I caused you and I'm going to try to straighten out. I was fighting and I threw the plastic bed at Mickey. Mommy told me to go to bed. I gave her a bad time. I'm not mad that you hit me because I knew it was for my own good. I want to go out a lot but I know that this letter will not make up for what I did. I will never cause any further trouble at home or at school. I hope that you change your mind about keeping Annie and me in the house.

Freddy

p.s. I'm chicken to say this to your face.

When I read the letter my father had written in response to Fred, I was surprised; it showed the understanding and humor he often failed to express.

Dear chicken,

Freddy, I did not know that it was a plastic bed you threw at Mickey. I thought it was the kitchen sink. Please stop giving Mommy a bad time for your own good. Don't think this letter is the cincher, but you can go out. But be careful and do as you're told. Tell Annie it's okay, too.

See you later,

Chicken's Dad

Staten Island, New York
Mid-1970's

I had not been home long from my training in the French Alps as an instructor of Transcendental Meditation when I heard the knock at our front door that would soon lead to my next great adventure. It was a Saturday afternoon in 1976, an unusual day in that our entire family of six was home and in the kitchen at the same time. We had been gathered around the table, talking to Fred about his newly-diagnosed cancer, when one of our childhood friends from the South Beach projects and St. Sylvester's School, Adele Harrigan, arrived at our home. No one

154

had known she was coming to visit, and so it was quite a shock to see her for the first time in 20 years. Pleasantries were exchanged. We all found our way around the table; we had coffee and got caught up on the last two decades. Then we discovered the reason for her unexpected visit. She wanted to talk to my father about the curse that had overcome her life: alcohol. As it had been an all-too-familiar reason for visitors to sit at our table, the rest of us found a way, as was customary, to excuse ourselves from the kitchen to allow for talk we had no need to hear.

Like most of us from that generation, Adele had begun drinking early and never stopped. Her father, John, used to drink with my father; they would often spend their time and paychecks at a local watering hole called Club Trio. Poorly lit and air laden with the smell of stale beer, the bar was always crowded with working-class types and a number of mobsters from the predominantly Italian neighborhood. John had spent his life burdened by the company he kept with alcohol. Sadly, an overconsumption of alcohol was a pattern to be followed later by a number of his seven children. Adele was his sixth child, but she was the first to seek relief from addiction. Growing up, her home environment had been yet another tale of unhinged family life. Theirs was a family atmosphere more of turmoil than violence, always intensified by the ever-demanding needs of seven children.

A smart, attractive, and hard-working woman, Adele's lifestyle had become untenable. For the last 15 years, she had managed to conduct, to all appearances, an advancing (if not unpredictable) lifestyle infused with alcohol and Valium. Now she sat across the table from Mean Mike in search of liberation from that lifestyle. While my father quietly listened, she shared the story of insanity that had forced her to make a change. She pointed out all the problems she faced in her life. When she was done speaking, my father told her – as he told all the countless alcoholics he had counseled over the years – that she only had one problem: alcohol. "Take care of that problem and all the others will disappear."

Undeterred by his generally forceful introduction to recovery and hopeful of change for the better, Adele agreed to follow whatever course of action he prescribed. Unbeknownst to Mean Mike at the time, she was always armed with a loaded pistol to ward off whatever fear the day might conjure. To varying degrees, fear was always present for the alcoholic. Uncertainty, amplified by strained emotions, would often elicit overreactions to simple situations. For Adele, her gun acted as a counterbalance. She may have been unassuming to the eye; but she was, in fact, as my father would say, "a real piece of work."

Just as my father's greatest day was the day he met my mother, so, too, it was for me when I became reacquainted with our childhood friend, Adele. She and my sister soon became close friends as they now shared the common bond of sobriety. Annie, having made her own passage from drinking after reaching her proverbial low point in life some few years earlier, was a shining example that there was hope of overcoming addiction. In the course of their renewed friendship, Annie asked if I would be willing to give Adele a hand painting some rooms in her newly-rented house. I agreed, unknowingly taking the first step toward our courtship.

Our uncomplicated attraction and the ease of our communication quickly strengthened our love for one another. We were married within a year. Up until that point in my life, I had lived like a vagabond; for years, I had been chasing creative dreams in hopes of hitting it big. Although subdued by marriage, those creative juices still flowed within me – they were simply part of my nature – but I knew it was time to begin anew. Starting a family on Staten Island, we soon had two sons and a growing desire to leave the burgeoning population of New York behind. With two children in tow, we moved to Pennsylvania. I started a painting business with a friend, a Vietnam veteran like myself seeking an opportunity to escape the city for a quieter life in the mountains. We established ourselves and did okay businesswise, but I soon found myself needing another change.

Texas
Mid-1980's

Filled with an ever-enduring optimism, my wife and I decided to relocate to Texas to be closer to my sister. After having had surgery for breast cancer (and as far as we knew, now in remission), Annie had moved to Texas to live for a short time with Clara, the psychic who had once lived with us on Staten Island. They had been working together for several years, traveling the country doing psychic readings. Annie had always possessed an insightfulness that was strangely prophetic. She would play down her abilities as nothing out of the ordinary; but, while living with us on Richmond Road, Clara had become acutely aware of my sister's abilities. When Annie finally approached her for guidance, Clara had welcomed the opportunity to help her refine her talent. Over time, they developed a very strong bond.

Now living alone, Annie was able to put us up until we could find our own place. She was thrilled that we were there with her. Sadly, we had been there only ten days when she suddenly became seriously ill and was admitted to the hospital. Unbeknownst to us, she had been battling an aggressive resurgence of her cancer. Ever strong in the face of adversity, Annie assured us she would be out in a couple of days, but her condition took a turn for the worse: her cancer had metastasized and her prognosis was not good. In meeting with her doctor, we learned that she had but some few weeks to live. His words skirting emotion, but not without feeling, were sharp, decisive, and heart-wrenching: "I wish that I had better news, but there is nothing further we can do. I'm sorry." It was one of those helpless moments where everything comes to a standstill; we were suspended in shock, devastated by the news. It was, in a word, painful.

My wife and I, along with Clara, set about trying to make Annie as comfortable as possible once she was admitted to the hospital. Annie, in turn, encouraged us not to feel the pain that was clear on our faces, providing us reassurance that she was at peace with what was to come. The courage that rose from her convictions shielded her from fear and brought comfort to those around her. I marveled at her strength, wondering if I could ever be so strong in the face of such predictable uncertainty. We took turns spending as much time with her as possible. All the while, she maintained her sense of humor. The days passed slowly as she drew closer to her exodus, her consciousness gradually fading. Shorter were our conversations; longer were her periods of sleep. Each time I left her bedside and exited the hospital into the powerful Texas sun, I felt guilty for my own good health. I was keenly aware of that precious, most times overlooked, state of equilibrium in the body that supports us through this life. Fortunate are those in good health, for they hold an unrecognized blessing – a blessing unlike any other.

My mother and father joined us in Texas to share with Annie the final days of her life. We surrounded her with our love and prayed for a comfortable transition. All the while, she kept assuring us that everything would be okay. I was troubled by the pain I sensed in my parents. Here was another of their children preparing to leave this earth before them; they already lived with the attendant aching memory of the loss of my brother. The loss of a child, nonetheless two children, was a pain recognized universally as one no progenitor of life should ever experience.

If my sister would find peace when her life concluded, then her passing – her deliverance – would be an acceptable and welcomed event. Embracing death as it draws near is as powerful a challenge as avoiding it throughout life. Knowing that her time had arrived and with her spiritual arms wide open, my sister of 35 years left her body on the evening of July 15, 1986 to join those awaiting her as her journey continued. Death is a painful blessing when it finally relieves the suffering of those lingering on the threshold of the great unknown. It brings a relative finality unlike anything else. Slowly quieting the senses, the mind, and, at last, the heart, the shell that houses our soul completes its role.

Annie's final service was small, a simple tribute paid to her life. Our dear friend Clara provided us with cherished insights regarding the events occurring unseen by us: family members, friends, and a host of others were accompanying Annie's now-liberated spirit, providing solace and welcoming hands. Our mourning for Annie may have been unconventional, but a more sincere and heartening service I have not attended. My parents brought Annie's ashes to Staten Island where they were scattered around a tree planted in her memory in a wooded area that she was fond of. My sister lived a life amidst challenges similar to those many of us face, but her spirited commitment to live life fully and without condemnation of its trials was a testament to her strength of character. Her smile, laughter, and goodwill are always missed when something stirs her memory within me.

***

We had been in Texas for only a month and were experiencing a very rocky beginning on our road to a fresh start. As fate would have it, 1986 was a very bad time to be looking for work in Texas. The price of oil had plummeted and the real-estate market had collapsed; we had also seen the first bank closure since the Great Depression. With two kids and another due in five short months, finding work became a difficult task and a growing concern.

Adele handed me a newspaper one morning and said, "You have to read this article on stress." The article highlighted the leading causes of stress in a family's life: the loss of a loved one, moving, being unemployed, pregnancy, financial difficulties, and eviction. We were experiencing each and every one, right down to the eviction. Immediately after we lost Annie, her landlord had wasted no time in moving us along. So things were, in a word, bad. We struggled for some months to try to regain our psychological and financial balance. I did whatever I could to make a buck; among other ventures, I sold insurance, real estate, and limited partnerships for oil drilling projects.

The most interesting job I held involved taking care of a small herd of horses. I had met with the owner of a small ranch in response to an ad in the paper looking for someone to care for around 30 horses and some other livestock. The owner turned out to be an eccentric psychiatrist; her horses turned out to be Arabians. I knew next to nothing about horses, and I said so; but I also made it clear that I was reliable and willing to learn. My enthusiasm and sincerity, along with the mention that I had two kids and another on the way, got me the job. I soon learned the horses I was to care for were extremely valuable – just one of the studs she owned was worth $40,000. Their value gave me a new view of my charge, and so I did my best to attend to their needs. I had never before been so closely acquainted with horses, but I discovered them to be majestic animals. I understood why they had been prized by man throughout the ages: they were beautiful, graceful, and powerful. I enjoyed tending to them so much that I even gave them my own nicknames. On occasion I would bring my five- and seven-year-old boys with me to ride on the tractor as I carried around hay. All was going well until I came to feed the horses one afternoon only to find the gate to their pasture wide open – all the horses were gone. *Holy shit!* I frantically made my way around the property before I finally found all the horses huddled together in their new-found freedom. Unsure of how I would get them all back to their pasture, I decided to lure them with buckets of molasses and oats. I approached slowly, buckets in hand, talking to them calmly. Once I had their attention, I turned to head back to their pasture, all the while dropping the molasses and oats like in a scene from Hansel and Gretel. Surprisingly, all the horses followed and, in no time, I had them all secured. For a city boy in Texas, it was quite an experience. I was more than relieved that I would not have to explain to my employer why several hundred thousand dollars of horses were missing.

Our move to Texas simply had not gone as planned. After struggling through a rough two years, we decided to return to Pennsylvania. Years later we would often reflect on our time in

160

the Lone Star State, and, whenever times got tough, we would always say to each other, "It's no worse than Texas."

Staten Island, New York
Early 1990's

My father was the type of person who you thought would live forever; but, alas, he left this world in the year of his 73rd birthday. Of life he would say, "It's a paradox. Death is the key to bringing a true understanding of life so it gives you something to look forward to." Fearless in so many ways while masking his sensitive and vulnerable emotions, he left, as we all will, his own indelible mark on this world.

He had long suffered from bouts of vertigo, the result of the severe inner ear injury he had suffered after being bombed by the Japanese in New Guinea during his service in World War II. In the course of a routine exam, it was determined that he had an aortic aneurysm. Surgery was recommended and, soon after, performed in a New York City hospital. Although he had served as a surgical assistant in field hospitals while in the Pacific, my father had always been opposed to surgery unless it was the absolute last resort. Given the option of surgery, he felt you should always turn it down. "Never let them cut you," he would often say. He was not very fond of doctors and seemed to enjoy breaking their balls every chance he got: "A lot of these guys need to be challenged and have their egos deflated once in a while." My father was very good at doing just that. He felt "cutting" (as he described surgery) had become more of a money maker for doctors and, in many instances, was not always necessary. Given the severity of his condition, however, he reluctantly had to agree to the surgery. The outcome, somewhat prophetic, was the thing he feared most: during the routine procedure, he suffered a stroke. The extent of the damage was not all that clear at first. After some time in recovery, however, we were told it was worse than they expected: he could not speak and had lost his mobility. Isolated amidst the world of activity surrounding him, my father was now a muted and motionless witness to life.

It was a painful experience to see him once he was placed on a ward. Deprived of the ability to speak, I could see the anguish in his eyes. It seemed to be even worse if anyone other than my mother, my wife, or me were present. As he was unable to write or otherwise communicate, we had to rely on a 'yes' or 'no' system in the form of blinking to get some sense of his desires; his frustration with the process was clearly visible on his face. To see someone who had been so vocal throughout his lifetime now unable to perform the most basic function of speech was disheartening – it was a condition of the worst sort.

His dispirited awareness reached out through his eyes, speaking with a burning desire to be set free, as he lingered in the body that was no longer his own for nearly a month. Then his condition worsened: he slipped into a coma. We were told he had but some few days left to live. The doctor proposed a feeding tube to extend his life; but my mother and I both knew, without a shadow of a doubt, my father would have none of that. He would want to be released from his pain, not to have his existence prolonged in the undignified condition to which he had been reduced. Having concluded that all of the life-enhancing procedures available could only, at best, promote this vegetative state, I knew he would have rejected the feeding tube; I told the doctor as much.

His attending physician was shocked by our decision not to insert a feeding tube. Her response nearly set me off into a rage. Devoid of emotion and without sensitivity, she said, in a stinging fashion, "Well, you'll be killing him." As angered as I was by her callous response, I tried to calmly explain to her who my father was and how aware my mother and I were of what his wishes would be on the matter.

I was once told that the word *euthanasia* comes from the Greek word meaning *the good death*, but now being presented with the thought of euthanasia was troubling as it was not something I had considered up to this point. It is a type of decision that no one wants to be faced with, one that would long endure in the minds of those who bring it to bear, regardless of the circumstances. Yet in this situation – with a clear understanding of what my father would want, and in consideration of his prognosis and the futility of continued treatment – we would have been remiss if we did not choose to discontinue procedures that would simply keep his body alive. We had arrived at the painful, inescapable position of having to determine the continuance of life for our loved one.

My mother and I took turns at my father's bedside, relieved from our watch on occasion by friends who would arrive for an unexpected visit. One night while I sat vigil, I read to him from Kahlil Gibran, a poet he enjoyed. As he was no longer conscious, I both asked and answered questions. Our relationship, decades in the making, was slowly reaching an end. I reflected about our lives as father and son – the years, the emotions, and our experiences together in this life, both good and bad. Our bond was gradually dissolving before me. From this point on, there would be no more history between us; what we had in the past was all that would be. I told him I loved him – simple words that had never been exchanged between us.

While I sat in quiet contemplation late into the evening, in the dim light, I sensed a gathering of our lineage present in the room. The entire room seemed to be filling with the energy, names, and faces of those long lost, most never even known to me in this lifetime. Surely his own father and those before him would offer my father a welcoming hand when his time finally came. He stood on the edge of this life and at the doorstep of the next with all of us, living and deceased, by his side. I thought of my older brother, Fred, and my sister, Annie, who had both too soon completed their time on Earth. As I shared with them an inner, heartfelt conversation, I could feel their presence bringing me comfort; together we shared some parting moments with our father. On occasion during that night, I felt free enough to let my emotions drain forth from my eyes, a process I had all too often avoided. My tears, the concentrate of my thoughts, seemed to carry the sadness from my body in a natural, liberating course. I sat quietly with my father and celebrated his life with our unseen guests, knowing deep inside that all was well and in keeping with what must be.

After a few hours' respite the next afternoon, I returned to the hospital with my mother. Not only did we discover my father had been transferred to another room, but we saw that he now had a feeding tube. Despite our wishes to the contrary and without any further dialogue after our initial consultation, the doctor had made her own choice. Whether her decision was based on law or ethics, I did not know as we never got that far in our previous discussion on the matter; regardless, I was angry by what I saw as an end-run around our feelings.

Some few hours after expressing my displeasure with the doctor's decision, my mother called with the news that my father had drawn his last breath. She had been by his side. She told me he had opened his weary eyes, filled with the need for relief, and she told him it was okay to go; with that, my father of 44 years closed his eyes and left this life. I was saddened by his death but, at the same time, relieved to know he would no longer suffer the indignity of dwelling silently within the shell that was once his body. Our lives would not be the same without him.

***

My father had always been very clear about his acceptance of death as a welcomed experience. "It is a consequence of life," he would say. At times he even seemed to flirt with death, to unconsciously tempt fate as a way of then knowing what lay beyond the millennium of conjecture about what happens when our lives end. On a distorted philosophical basis, in an attempt to provoke such a debate, he once publicly posed the question "What does it feel like to be dead?" An odd question to be sure, all the more so when debated between inebriated construction workers in a workingman's bar on Manhattan's East Side.

It was a rainy day in Manhattan, and so the construction job my father was on had ceased work for the day. The bar seemed a logical place for him and his coworkers to seek shelter from the rain. As the day wore on, and after several hours of drinking, my father and his associates began sharing their spiritual insights, wondering aloud how one would feel when dead. Some conclusions were disregarded, while others inspired awe and acquiescence. Roundly intoxicated, they sought a better understanding than they were able to provide one another by virtue of sheer imagination. In a stroke of genius from one altered mind, it was proposed that they find out for themselves: "I know a guy who works at the New York City Morgue. We should go down there; climb into one of those drawers where they keep the stiffs and see for ourselves what it feels like." The idea was unanimously accepted. After a phone call to this friend at the morgue, and bolstered by a few more shots and beers, the group of spiritual researchers grabbed a taxi and headed for the repository of the dead.

Excited by their drunken goal, but not yet knowing exactly what to expect, the group reveled in their quest. It was dark and rainy when they arrived at the morgue. Pleasantries were exchanged with their inside accomplice – who thought they were completely nuts – before they were ushered to the depths of the morgue. A wall of refrigerated boxes awaited them in a tiled room, poorly-lit and filled with stainless steel gurneys. At this point there was some wavering of conviction by these adventurers as the reality of where they were began to set it. This room did not receive many visitors. Despite the reluctance of his comrades, my father went straightaway when asked by the morgue employee, "Who's first?" He grabbed the heavy latch without hesitation and pulled; the big drawer came creaking out on its metal bearings.

"Go ahead. Hop in." My father obliged their accomplice, securing his position in the cold metal container. "All set?"

"Yeah, go ahead," my father replied confidently.

"Bang when you want to come out."

With that, my father was pushed into the darkness, where only the dead had gone before. After a few brief moments of reflection, his experiment was complete. He banged on the cold metal door and was quickly brought back to the world of the living, as though reborn. Asked how it was, he simply said, "Dark." The empirical evidence was satisfying, and no one else chose to confirm his findings with their own spiritual journey. As they left the morgue, they thanked the employee for his assistance. They grabbed a taxi to return to the bar where they concluded their discussion of death and celebrated their meaningful, esoteric experiment.

***

We had my father cremated. While attending his wake, his friend Charlie approached me and said, "Hey, Mick, I would like to get a picture of your dad. I would also like to see the ashes in the urn to give a final goodbye." I was truly taken by surprise with the request. I told him the picture would not be a problem, but the ashes were sealed; not only would they be difficult to open but "I think it would freak out a lot of people if I open the urn." Although opening the urn seemed an odd request, I knew that, to Charlie, it was heartfelt, simple, and innocent. I was touched by his genuine, open affection for my father. I felt bad that I couldn't comply, but he understood.

***

Some 21 years after my father passed away, I would attend Charlie's own funeral. I would see his grown children who had often times accompanied him to our house while he visited with my father. I would also be shocked, but somehow not surprised, to see on a table displaying his family pictures, a 9.5x11" color portrait of my father – the very same picture used for my father's wake. In speaking with Charlie's wife, I would learn that he had kept that picture on his bedroom dresser for all of those 21 years. On one corner of the picture was a small note that read "Keep smiling." It was a saying my father frequently repeated, and one that always followed any goodbye he would utter. In a way I believe Charlie had seen Mean Mike as a father

166

figure: someone who had shared friendship and emotional support, someone who believed in him, someone who bolstered his self-confidence and his feeling of self-worth. After the funeral I would talk, at length, with his daughter and wife only to learn further that Charlie was buried with his beloved portrait of my father.

"Did you know he was buried with your father's picture?"

"No, I didn't."

"Oh yeah," said his wife with a smile, half serious and half joking, "and guess what? My picture is not in there."

It was quite a tribute, one that I thought my father and Charlie would both laugh about once they were reunited. It may have never been apparent on the surface, but I found it heartwarming to know they shared such a deep, long-standing friendship.

***

There was a long procession of familiar faces at my father's wake. Some had long lost the countenance of addiction, while others were still conveying the pain of battle. Taking the time to talk with them all, I realized my father had been at his best when he was able to serve others. One of those in attendance, a man who had known my father for some time, asked if he might speak. In his hand he held a paper listing what he called "Moynerisims," sayings that my father had developed over the years and had used frequently in the process of making a point (many of which people never fully understood):

You are some piece of work. (Derived from Shakespeare)

You don't know who you are.

Get the bag off your head.

Don't tell me who you are. What you are speaks so loudly I can't hear what you're saying.

Keep smiling.

Go to a meeting.

Don't take any wooden nickels.

Be good to yourself.

Most men lead lives of quiet desperation. (Thoreau)

Stop feeling sorry for yourself.

The only real problem in your life is drinking.

You are a real shit-head.

Stand up on the chair and we'll throw sugar at you. (I, personally, never understood this one.)

My father had no final wishes regarding where he wanted to be buried. He would often say, jokingly, "When I die, just bury me someplace in the backyard on Richmond Road." He wasn't fond of cemeteries; in fact, he referred to them as marble orchards. His irreverence for organized religion and traditional resting places left us wanting to respect his feelings while, at the same time, to provide a respectful home for his cremated remains. My brother Jimmy, who was living with my mother, found it intolerable to live with my father's ashes in the house. He had a long-standing hypersensitivity to wakes and funerals after being forced by the nuns at St. Sylvester's to attend the funeral of a young classmate; the experience had haunted him for years. So, my mother asked me to hold on to the ashes.

Some people place the ashes of loved ones on mantles or scatter them over land or water in fulfillment of the wishes of the departed. As my father had left no such wishes, I determined his ashes would find their home in his favorite car. I had inherited his beloved Chevy, and so I drove his ashes around in that car for 1-½ years. It was a resting place like no other – strange, yet appropriate. I felt no disrespect to him; in fact, I actually felt closer to him for it. But I finally decided that, as a veteran, a more honorable location for his final resting place would be in a national cemetery.

I set about securing a place for my father in the Indiantown Gap National Cemetery in Annville, Pennsylvania. One of dozens of such cemeteries maintained by the federal government and reserved for veterans and their spouses, my father had now found an honorable resting place here in a quiet and dignified setting. It was a small observance, a modest but thorough celebration of his life complete with a 21-gun salute from a local VFW post and followed by a bugler playing taps. Only 24 notes long, the sorrowful musical score of taps was his final ceremonial goodbye; that melody always made me melancholy as it reminded me of the fallen with whom I had served. The remains of his turbulent physical life had now come to rest alongside thousands of his fellow veterans and soldiers who had sacrificed their lives – by virtue of all that sacrifice entailed – in the name of our country. There was no pretentious competition here in marble or rank: no race or religion; no rich or poor; privileged or ordinary. The setting spoke with only one voice: We are Americans.

My mother and I both felt he would be happy here. We observed how the small, simple granite stones that marked each veteran's grave ran like rhythmic topographic lines, unending as they adjusted to the changing contours of the beautiful, well-maintained land. Some of the millions who had served and died in the military during World War II occupied a disproportionate number of the gravesites. Moving amidst the memories of their markers, I felt my father's colleagues now kept guard all around him. I felt a strong sense of pride for our country and for my father's service to it. I felt he had known very little of peace in this life, and so I prayed he would rest in peace here. As I lingered above his marker, I could not help but wonder about all that he had discovered once he had moved on from this life; he was surely relieved of the questions he had always quietly sought to answer. My father, always filled with surprises, still speaks to me through the things I see and do from the cultured genetic prism that endures inside me.

***

My mother came across an Army newsletter from November of 1941 while she was going through some of my father's things. She showed it to me and shared the story that went along with it. At 21 years of age, my father had been in a medical training battalion in Camp Lee, Virginia. Like so many of the patriotic young men of that time, he had a limited understanding of how things worked in the military. After arriving at Camp Lee, he had found his way to the enlisted men's club where he was able to acquire draft beer. Much to his delight, he was informed he did not have to pay for the beer; he simply had to tell the barkeep who he was. At the time he felt that this was a great perk for being in the Army, and so he drank his fill whenever he could. Unbeknownst to him, however, he had been running up a tab; and, by the time he received his first Army paycheck, he was told that he owed the government $0.25.

East Stroudsburg, Pennsylvania
Early 2000's

As far back as I can remember, my brother Jimmy was just a little different from everyone else. Always aware, quiet, and pleasant, he was never a problem, but there was always something that just didn't seem right with him: from a young age, he always seemed to be lagging behind in whatever he did. In the 1950's, "slow" was an umbrella expression, a way of covering a vast number of problems without giving particular importance to any specific one. Schoolchildren who were described as being slow did not receive a lot of attention. If students had a serious problem, they were segregated from their classmates. In most cases, however, slow students remained mainstreamed; such was the case with Jimmy. His motor skills were seen as lacking, and there were some cognitive deficiencies that made the world of education difficult for him. Mainstreamed with us at St. Sylvester's School, the nuns did their best to usher him through eight years of elementary education despite their limited resources for dealing with children who had learning problems. He was left back a couple of times, but eventually moved forward.

Jimmy had an unusual sense of humor that would crop up from time to time. When he was in the third grade, the nun teaching his class decided they would have a show and tell. Everyone was asked to bring something in the next day and to be ready to get up in front of the class to talk about what they had brought with them. He was frantic that afternoon when he came home from school; his worst fear, that of getting up in front of the class, would be realized. My mother, always creative and resourceful, helped him come up with an idea. She would make a sock puppet for Jimmy to bring to school; he could say it was one of his friends. Jimmy named the puppet Henry. He went to school with something to talk about: a sock puppet whose features were created by buttons. He was confident that, being one of 40 kids in the class, it was unlikely he would have to speak; however, much to his dismay, Sister Carmelita began the show and tell by calling Jimmy to the front of the class first. Shocked, paralyzed, and overcome with anxiety, he was ushered to the dreaded space at the front of the room to present Henry. As he nervously slipped the sock over his hand, Sister Carmelita asked Jimmy to tell the class something about his puppet: "Tell us his name. Does he have anything to say?" Red in the face and squirming uneasily, Jimmy managed to utter the words, "His name is Henry." After enduring a long pause as Jimmy wished he were somewhere else, anywhere else, Sister Carmelita once again asked if Henry had anything to say. In a moment of desperation, Jimmy told the class, in no uncertain terms, that Henry had laryngitis. He then quickly made his way back to his seat.

Moving along through the world at his own pace, difficult though it might have been, Jimmy managed his way through high school and into the workplace. His saving grace was a job that my wife, Adele, secured for him in a mailroom with Deutsche Bank in New York City. He was slow to the job at first; but once he developed a routine and familiarity with the city while delivering bonds and mail, he became the most reliable of workers. He took the responsibility of his job seriously. He never called in sick, never complained, and never made trouble; he just quietly did his job. He put years of service with the company behind him as he continued to live at home with my parents.

Jimmy seemed to come alive – to become noticeably animated – more when watching sports than at any other time. His life centered on sports, and he was a loyal fan of his beloved baseball team, the Mets. Vocal, excited, and exceptionally aware of what was going on with his favorite sport, he could cite batting averages, positions, and greatly-detailed history. In comparison to Jimmy's sports knowledge, I was ignorant.

In 2001, working very close to the World Trade Center in downtown Manhattan, Jimmy's world (along with the worlds of so many others) was changed forever on the fateful September morning of 9/11. He found himself in the midst of a kind of chaos that he had not known before; the sensitivity of his nature and the way he saw things certainly heightened this experience of sheer terror for him. His life had been built upon regularity, comfortable repetition, and predictability; in a moment all of that was gone, and he found himself living a nightmare.

That very morning I sat quietly on my front porch. I was comfortable, secure, and content, drinking a morning cup of coffee and reading the paper. The moment had the essence of a Norman Rockwell painting. I was unaware of what had taken place moments ago – only 90 miles away – in New York City, when a meter reader for a local utility disrupted my quiet setting. We acknowledged each other's presence with a nod. Then, after saying, "Good morning," he asked if I had heard what happened. "A commercial jet just crashed into one of the World Trade Center towers in Manhattan. I just heard about it on the radio in my truck." He went on to say that there seemed to be a great deal of confusion as to how something like this could have happened on such a clear, sunny morning. I thanked him for the information, swallowed the last gulp of my coffee, and went inside to turn on the television. There was no shortage of information, both live and prerecorded, about the events that were unfolding. I immediately thought of Jimmy; he was in and out of those buildings every day in the course of his work. *My God, it's Tuesday!* That meant my mother would also be in Lower Manhattan for the volunteer work she did at a hospital on a weekly basis. I kept trying to reach them both by phone, but my efforts were useless; all lines were down. I moved from channel to channel on the television, trying to gather as much information as I could. Each station was airing the burning tower live on the screen, with an endless flow of commentary and speculation. The tower burned like a huge smoldering silver torch; smoke swirled above the centurion structure, bellowing from its interior and filling the sky with artificial clouds and debris. It created a shadowy darkness over the city that would linger long after the smoke had cleared. That darkness would fill the homes of families far beyond the borders of our country. It was a darkness that would become part of our national history – part of who we are as a people and what directs us in our decisions, both domestic and foreign.

I could only wonder where my family members were amidst the throngs of people flooding the streets, all fleeing from something ominous, yet still unknown. Things became clearer as things grew worse: when a second plane struck the other tower, it was obvious the city was under attack. Powerful, earthshaking explosions filled the air with debris. Paper, thousands of sheets of paper, fell from the sky like messages from those above; each sheet slowly tossed by the wind as it fell to the streets below was a part of the story taking place. Masses of people were pouring from the towers and surrounding buildings; horror and disbelief covered their faces as primal instinct moved them away from the source of fear. My attention was riveted to the TV as the dreadful sight of people in distress played out for all to see; this landscape of disaster was being shared in real time with the world.

Once again I could only wonder where my mother and brother were amidst the chaos of this evolving disaster. I sat helplessly with my phone in hand, continuing to hit 'redial' over and over again without any luck of getting a connection. The thought had even occurred to me that I might try to drive into the city to find them; then I heard it announced that the tunnels and bridges to New York City had been closed for security reasons. Staring intently at the screen, I watched in utter disbelief as one of the towers then began to give way. Seeing each floor succumb to the weight of the ones above, building in momentum as they drew closer to the streets below, a chill went up my spine and hairs rose on the back of my neck; I began to register the loss occurring. Collapsing onto itself – splintering, folding, and disappearing from sight with a tremendous rumbling noise – the entire building was gone in some few moments. Amidst the rumbling I imagined the voices of those perishing calling out to their families with their last breathes; their final haunting calls echoing through the streets of downtown New York. The exponential level of sadness, grief, and loss felt by family, friends, and strangers as they witnessed the scene was palpable. The building had fallen like a soldier who had taken a mortal wound. No one in the streets a thousand feet below had been prepared for the deadly weight of that manmade mountain to shower them at its base. It was the stuff of wars, typically reserved to be seen by soldiers in battle – not to be consumed by tender hearts. These terrible, unavoidable, gripping scenes would last a lifetime in the memories of their beholders.

When the second tower fell, great bellowing clouds raced through the catacombs of the city streets. Like some biblical image on an ancient masters' canvass, those clouds seemed to possess the souls of the towers. Shrieking like banshees as they rumbled through lower Manhattan, those clouds carried with them the souls of those who had perished, escorting them on their journey to meet whatever fate their beliefs prescribed. These two silver pillars had been landmarks of the New York City skyline. They had served as centers for trade and finance, as a place of work for thousands in the greatest city in the world; and now they were no more. Their remains hidden beneath a shroud of smoke, these recently majestic, magnificent structures were suddenly gone from view and conspicuous by their absence.

A wave of humanity struggled to survive the harsh climate created by the fall of the towers. The raging soul-filled clouds that had stormed through the streets, propelled by some unseen force, had blanketed everything with a strange white powder like artificial snow. People were filling their lungs with air not meant to be breathed – poisoned air – as they traveled the streets in search of relief, accompanied by those who shared their fate. An enemy that would soon feel our country's great wrath for such a transgression had brought about this defenseless slaughter of innocents. Enraged that an enemy had found its way to our shores and provoked us in such an inhumane and cowardly way, I engaged in a gluttonous feed on the negativity served by the media. All the while, the tight grasp of uncertainty as to my family's whereabouts tightened its hold; I prayed for their well-being, hoping they had found safety.

The former site of the towers would forever forth be known as Ground Zero. Void of recognizable structures, the site was labeled with a name reserved for the locations of nuclear detonations; it was an appropriate indicator of what befell the eyes upon approach. Amidst the smoldering mass, firemen searching for their lost brothers came upon a lone flagpole that had survived the long fall from above in one piece. In a gesture of resolve in the face of an attack, and in respect to those fallen, the American flag was raised on that flagpole. It was a quiet, solemn, and respectful tribute to those who had perished. It also served as a reminder for those who lived on to pursue justice in our nation's name. The sight was eerily similar to the nationally-revered image of the Marines raising the flag on Mount Suribachi on the island of Iwo Jima during World War II, a war that had also begun after a sneak attack.

I remained captivated by the news coverage. I watched as first responders clawed their way across the steaming maze of twisted metal and concrete, searching feverishly for life in that deadly, foreign landscape. Some searched for friends and family, others for coworkers or no one in particular. Water was poured upon the volcano-like knoll in an attempt to still the fires that burned deep within. The surface remained so hot in spots that it melted the soles of the rescuers' shoes; yet they lifted, carried, and worked together in a task too large for human hands as they tore away at the desolate mountain in search of survivors. Hoping against all hope to find someone who might have survived, they would call out, listening for some responsive indication of life amidst the debris. Working through fatigue and well past the point of exhaustion, first responders continued into the night, unaware of the passage of time and the need to rest. Theirs was a job that knew no end.

In a world capable of instant communication, it was hard to comprehend that it took me several days before I could speak to my mother and brother. *Thank God, they are both all right.* My mother had safely made her way uptown, finding shelter at her sister's home on 34th Street. Jimmy, although very close to the towers at the time of their collapse, was also uninjured. He was traumatized, but he had managed to hurry through the chaos in lower Manhattan to make his way home across New York Harbor. He explained that an armada of boats of every description had been waiting on the shoreline to ferry people away from the city. Like those fleeing the eruption of Mt. Vesuvius, the sea offered safe passage. He managed his way onto a crowded tugboat to be returned to the safety of Staten Island. The overwhelming sentiments of the day had been anger and shock; ultimately, however, there was gratitude for surviving. My mother and brother, together with all New Yorkers, would never be the same.

***

Throughout the years I had kept in touch with my good friend Bob Hegler. Over time he had adjusted to his injuries from Vietnam and bought a home. Always imaginative, he had become a well-known stained glass artist. He worked from his home workshop, commercially designing custom stained glass windows. He seemed content with work that allowed for his creative spirit to be expressed through his hands; his love of art had always enhanced his deep appreciation for life.

Bob had also overcome the curse of addiction; his mentor in this process had been none other than Mean Mike. My father had known Bob for years, as he lived across the street from us, and was well aware that he suffered from an addiction to painkillers. Bob had developed the problem with drugs during the time he had spent in the Army hospitals while recovering from his war injuries. When he had finally managed to overcome his reliance on painkillers, alcohol stepped in and grew to become an even bigger problem. Like so many others, he had to look no further than his own family to see the lurking curse; known to all of his friends, his mother was a heavy drinker. I could truly feel Bob's embarrassment one night while a group of us (maybe 13 or 14 years of age at the time) were hanging around on our favorite neighborhood corner. From several blocks away, we noticed someone swerving toward us on a bicycle. As the rider drew closer, we saw that it was Bob's mom; she was drunker than hell. In one hand she managed a quart of beer; her other hand managed the steering. A humiliating cry sounded by one of our friends brought a look to Bob's face with which I was all too familiar: "Hey, Bob, here comes your mother. Man, is she drunk." His mother stopped to visit with her son and his friends for some few torturous moments before continuing on her unstable journey. It didn't take long for the callous humor of teenagers to find its way to Bob ears. The ridicule went on for some time; Bob could only endure that which he could not defend. It was one of those strikingly sad events that became fixed in the memory of the children of alcoholics. The alcoholic's family inevitably suffered collateral damage by association in the battle of addiction.

Known by those experienced with addiction, alcohol was more difficult to overcome than most drugs. It had taken some years before Bob was able admit to himself that alcohol had truly taken over his life and to seek help from my father. It was an awkward, rough road for both of them, partly because they already knew each other so well. Both very bright, stubborn, and lacking, at times, in the finesse of expressing an opinion of one another, they were an oil-and-water combination from the start. Bob would often bristle because of my father's no-nonsense insistence on a strict adherence to his rules for gaining sobriety, but they both persevered; over time they developed a mutual respect for one another. Bob had managed to overcome alcohol and became one of those fortunate enough to break his family's chain of addiction. In the tradition of AA, he then went on to help scores of others do the same.

One February morning in 2008, I received a call from Bob. In his characteristically impulsive way, he asked if I would be interested in taking a trip to Florida. It was a question that brought to mind our history of spontaneous travel together after Vietnam. Unfortunately, I knew there was an unspoken reason for Bob wanting to take this particular trip: it was to say goodbye. We had some old friends living in Florida; Bob said he just wanted to pay them a visit, but I knew better. Bob had been sick for some time, suffering from a degenerative brain disorder. His prognosis had recently worsened; he had been told he had but some few months to live. Like in my brother Fred's case, it had been suggested that his condition could have resulted from exposure to Agent Orange in Vietnam. It was yet another burden Bob had to endure from a war long past. Having overcome each obstacle he had encountered in life, he was now faced with one insurmountable; yet, in his distinctive embrace of whatever fate brought to him, Bob had set about readying himself for what was to come.

I told him, "Let me talk to my wife, and I'll call you back." Adele had known Bob for a long time; she was aware of his health situation. As I was now retired and our children were grown, she simply told me, "Sure, go ahead." I called Bob back to ask him when he wanted to leave. He said, "Soon would be good." I sensed the urgency in his response and told him I'd be ready in a few days.

***

I was happy Bob had called me to accompany him as he delivered his implicit goodbyes. I was also saddened by this new burden on top of all the other pain I had witnessed him deal with through so many years; his sharp intellect had always distinguished him from my other friends, and now he would quickly lose that as well. Bob's life had been tragic, filled with more sorrow than one man should have to endure. In addition to his injuries from Vietnam and his addictions, there was another particularly awful incident in Bob's life that had always troubled me. It had occurred while I was away at school in Iowa.

Bob's brother, John, had a long history of mental problems and was still living in their childhood home with their father. One day while his father was at work, Bob stopped by the house only to find the place in flames – his brother was inside. Our house was only a few doors down from Bob's, and so the sound of the sirens quickly brought my father out to the street. They could not gain entry because of the flames; they could only watch as the firemen tried to get the fire under control. It was then that they witnessed John running back and forth screaming behind the closed windows on the second floor. He perished in the fire. Bob was in a state of shock. My father, himself truly upset by what they had just witnessed, tried to provide him with what little comfort he could. It was an incident that surely haunted Bob for the remainder of his days.

***

We were on the road within a week. I had suggested to Bob that we might fly instead of driving all the way to Tampa, but he told me that flying had a peculiar effect on him. Given his condition, he said that he was better suited for driving. He asked me, "What kind of a road trip would it be if we are in an airplane?" So I rented a car and picked Bob up in New York to begin what I knew would be his last trip.

Just like our trip around the country 30 years earlier, we had no schedule or time constraints. While traveling south, we often got lost in reminiscing. We had both seen a lot of changes since our free-spirited trip in the 1970's, and so our drive time was filled with stories about our pasts. We had shared a lot of history together and both concluded that we could not have anticipated how things would have turned out. I could see that the travel and all the talk were wearing Bob out; I was happy when we finally arrived in Tampa. His spirit was revived once we connected with our old friends Larry and Lori. They had been made aware of his condition in advance of our arrival by some mutual friends. We spent several days together, laughing and telling stories about each other and how we looked now that we had grown older. As it was not his way, Bob never once made mention of the worsening of his condition; likewise, our hosts never let on that they knew what had prompted his visit and what was to come for him. We simply enjoyed our time together – a time we knew would never come again. When we readied ourselves to head back home, I watched as old friends said their goodbyes for the last time, left to face the inevitable. Their prolonged hugs seemed to last forever, somehow deepening the feeling not conveyed by their final parting words. Their embraces lasted some few powerful moments, acknowledging their friendship and the larger separation that was to come. As the tears of departure were wiped from their faces, they each secured parting gazes with Bob for the premature mental album of those departed. I was moved by the farewell.

Once on the road, we endured an awkward silence. It was as though a part of Bob had just perished. After some time he finally said, "I'm glad I got to see them." With those few words, I could feel how important this trip had been for him. I slowly returned from the morbid and intrusive thoughts that had been distracting me, and we began to entertain ourselves with the mundane talk of the road. Like most return trips, our trip home seemed long and subdued.

To pass the time during our drive, Bob and I would often recall quotes from songs that expressed certain sentiments, both happy and sad. We would interpret the music of our time as if we were doing the work of minstrels. "Wonder how tomorrow could ever follow today," "The times they are a-changing," "You say you want a revolution," "You can't always get what you want,"

"Excuse me while I kiss the sky," and "Four dead in Ohio" were the types of lyrics that led us into long discussions of their whimsical nature or true meaning. Songs evolve within every era that resonate and bring meaning and understanding to our lives. The music of our generation reflected the conflict, joy, spirituality, and optimism that were so much a part of the 1960's and 1970's. Our generation shared a birth in time, a life familiar, yet unique amongst the ages. We were an expression, a reawakening of the spiritual essence of man and nature; ours was a valuable contribution that arose from an otherwise chaotic period.

For Bob, the anticipation of our reunion was now replaced by the thought of doctors, tests, and what he knew awaited him in the not-too-distant future. *What do you say to someone who does not have long to live?* Words of concern or foreboding were not what he needed, nor wanted to hear. I think we both knew deep inside that, although his fate was determined, his impending death was a mystery not to be feared. Bob may not have been religious, but he was a deeply spiritual person. Familiar with most religions, he found himself drawn to Buddhism more than any other; he believed in reincarnation and the ways of karma. I realized that what he sought – especially from me – was to be treated as though nothing was out of the ordinary; in fact, it wasn't. The everyday concerns that surround our lives surely have less meaning for those living with the marked uncertainty of how many more days they can put behind them; yet it is those very concerns with which they need to occupy their minds. I looked at Bob and, unable to share my emotion, simply thought to myself, *I am proud to be your friend.*

There was an old Blues song that we used to listen to that I think best described Bob's life: "Born Under a Bad Sign." As the song went, "If it wasn't for bad luck, I wouldn't have no luck at all." I sincerely believe there is a connection with the cosmos at our birth which determines the quality and direction of our lives. Karmic cosmic connections surely must provide the threads and course of our existence. As bad as Bob's luck might have been, his life was meaningful in its influence on others. Having shared many difficult times with him myself, I learned a greater acceptance of the things in life that I cannot change. Never bitter about what life brought his way, Bob served as an inspiration for me. Demonstrating a way to a better life through both word and deed, he was also an inspiration to the many people he helped to recover from an addiction to alcohol.

Several weeks after our trip, a friend in New York called to inform me that Bob had been hospitalized. He was in a coma. I went to visit him and found his frail, wiry body putting up a last fight to simply draw air into his lungs. The openings in his hospital gown displayed the many wounds from war that his clothing had always concealed; we called them the tattoos of war, one-of-a-kind permanent reminders branded in flesh. His every breath was labored and rattled within his chest; each gasp was filled with the rasping prospect of being his last. Upon seeing him my eyes filled with tears, the fluid of sympathy, seeking to relieve my inner pain. Forty years earlier I had stood by his bedside as he lay in critical condition upon his return from Vietnam. Back then he had managed to survive insurmountable odds and overcome his injuries, but this time there would be no remarkable survival story. The outcome of the battle he now fought – the battle to live – had already been decided against him. Being there with him should have felt like the right thing to do, but I knew Bob; he would not want to be seen in that condition. Suddenly, feeling intrusive and knowing that I could bring no comfort to Bob or myself by being there, I respectfully spoke some few words of farewell to his deafened ears, hoping my sentiments might have registered somewhere within him.

My wife and I were scheduled to leave for a Florida vacation the next day. Shortly after arriving at our destination, I learned that Bob had passed away. I thought of my father, brother, and sister – all of whom were connected to Bob – all having passed in a similarly painful way. Now that his battle had come to an end, I felt a strange relief, a certain peace and a comforting awareness in knowing Bob was unburdened of his pain. Perhaps now he would somehow be given an understanding of what his troubled life had truly been all about.

I imagined he dwelled somewhere unseen, surrounded by friends, light, and peace. The sadness of his passing brought to mind a quote from General George S. Patton, a bold and controversial leader of World War II fame who loved his troops. He once said of those lost in battle, "It is foolish and wrong to mourn the men who died. Rather we should thank God that such men lived." Bob was a true warrior, a good man and a decent human being who had fought many battles in this life. While I continue to miss him, I have tried not to mourn his death.

Some months after Bob passed I received a call from his sister. She told me that she was going to spread his ashes on a lake in a park where he always enjoyed spending time; she wanted to know if I would accompany her and two other friends. I agreed and met them for what was to be a short, simple farewell. We found Bob's favorite spot in the park and took turns expressing our individual parting sentiments while spreading his ashes. As the physical remnants of his life were gradually absorbed into the lake, I began to feel at peace with his passing.

At some point in life, we each assume the role of a survivor; it is at times like this when we cannot help but be reminded of our own impermanence. Each of us will, at some point, be survived by someone else. A temporary role is that of a survivor.

***

Life is like a great painting that becomes more valuable over time, a painting begun never to be finished, to be viewed by those with the will to see. It is a spiritual canvas stretched across the vacuous reaches of all that is, with all-too-real lifelike scenes of what is and what shall be. Telling a story started long ago, life is a document of immeasurable proportions. Scenes of joy and sorrow fill the greatest of celestial landscapes, painted with endless contrast of scale and color; light and dark are woven through the universe, spilling forth from the Creator's astral brush. Nothing escapes the eye of the artist. Stellar, artistically expressing the vision, desire, and power of the painter, each stroke portrays an eon complete in detail. I look upon this painting reverently, with eyes that have gained knowledge over many years. As my vision has evolved, my contemplation of its beauty and its meaning has grown stronger. Inadequate are my words to express my appreciation or to describe what the artist had in mind. *How does a master begin his greatest work? Was it a dream, a reverie, a fanciful intention ages in its musing that brought this unending work to be? What stroke would commence that which will never end? What mood, if any, is befitting a Creator while He labors at His masterpiece, His self-portrait?*

***

Despite my best efforts, I was never fully repatriated from war; there was always something inside of me that remained out of balance. As I faithfully carried out my duties as a husband, father, and citizen, I always felt as though I was trying to keep one step ahead of something that pursued me – a faceless antagonist that perpetually disrupted my inner peace. Seeking to engage me with a shameless display of its misappropriated scrapbook of my traumatic past, that antagonist was relentless in its pursuit. Transcendental Meditation had been instrumental in neutralizing many of the negative habits I had developed – it had brought me a positive, reassuring outlook on life – but it had not truly changed me. Conformity to most social norms remained a challenge; something of myself remained absent from my life. The realization that my life was not quite right and the will to do something about it came only after two decades of intense personal struggle.

It was implied, if not expected, by my father's generation to simply accept haunting memories as the price of war. Many veterans of World War II silently carried their pain all the way to their grave. Like my father and brother before me, I, too, had been quietly battling the demons of war. To all appearances, except to those close to me, I was normal; in reality, many were the internal conflicts with which I struggled. I often reigned victorious over an unseen enemy as I confronted imagined armies on different fronts over the course of those 20 years, but there can be no ultimate victory in a war with the unknown. The harpies I would think I had vanquished always managed to return to my mind's field of battle, incessantly contributing to my conceptual fatigue. Some days proved peaceful by virtue of an undeclared armistice, but most nights proved dark and disturbed. When I would close my eyes to retreat from a conscious state and enter the world of dreams, it seemed all things ill-conceived were possible; regular encounters with real-life fears preyed upon my defenseless mind. My psyche was like a blank screen, and I the director who had lost control of his script to those who sought to haunt me. I often wondered how long I could continue to relive my traumas...apparently forever. My father had once told me, and rightfully so, that "the images of war would be with you for the rest of your life."

I had always believed that acknowledging difficulty would diminish my sense of self. Now requiring help for being who I had become significantly tarnished my sense of pride; and so it was with great reluctance that I sought out the Veterans Administration (VA) to address my concerns. I knew I would be beginning another long, and oftentimes disappointing, battle; this was a battle I had hoped to avoid.

The VA had long been established in its role as protector of the veteran; that was what I now had to rely on. After testing and consultations with psychiatrists, I started treatment for post-traumatic stress disorder (PTSD). My inability to stay with any one job for an extended period of time, along with my anger, flashbacks, nightmares, hyper vigilance, and a long list of other symptoms, made for an uncomplicated initial evaluation. My father had never been fond of the technicians of the mind; in fact, he referred to them as "the head shrinkers." Although he had shared no specific information about his own interaction with them, I'm sure he had been evaluated before leaving the service. Whenever the subject of psychiatrists would arise in the treatment of alcoholism, he would say, "They're all fuckin' nuts, and all they want to do is give you pills to make everything all right." While being counseled, I would find myself trying to censure the growing parallels I discovered between myself and my father. I may have been his son, but I thought that I was far more reserved than he was when it came to the expression of my darker side.

Upon seeing no appreciable improvement after a few years of working with the VA, I decided to seek help from private counselors. Counsel outside of the VA system proved more to my liking. The VA doctors had always seemed overworked and preoccupied, creating what I sensed to be an atmosphere of indifference. Vietnam was a guerilla war that had left its own special mark on those who fought. This war had cycled troops through the Southeast Asian jungles year after year, thereby creating an overwhelming number of those who needed help and challenging the ability of our country to adequately support them. Expressing a disengaged and disrespectful *"Who's next? mentality"* to the endless lines of those seeking help, never before had our country so divorced itself from its duty in caring for its defenders.

In the course of my interaction with the VA, it was suggested that I apply for compensation for both the physical injuries I had sustained in Vietnam and for the PTSD with which I now lived. At first, like so many others, I was reluctant to seek out an evaluation of my claims, acknowledging that there were so many more veterans in worse shape than myself. Over time, however, I came to realize that my claims were sound and unselfish. I only wanted what I was entitled to as a veteran – nothing more, but nothing less. So began an arduous journey of headaches and aggravation as I worked my way through the great bureaucracy of the Veterans Administration. As have many veterans, I felt a sense of apathy from those with whom I dealt. Whether it was because of the nature of an insensitive bureaucracy with its attending never-to-be-fired personnel or just the volume of claimants and the time needed to process them, the system was lacking in both compassion and efficacy.

When I came across one of the rating charts used by the VA to equate loss with compensation, I was further struck by what I saw as the impersonal nature of the administration. All of my concerns, problems, and disabilities had been rounded out to the nearest decimal to achieve a dollar figure – completely depersonalized. Such was the process that spanned the course of months (which turned into years) with its continued requests for documentation, examination, submittals, reviews, and board decisions; and then there were the appeals, for no one ever seemed to get what they deserved after the first request for compensation. The process was disheartening, humiliating, and insensitive, but my determination was full. I would see through to the end what had become, in my eyes, a test of will with this slow-moving, emotionless agency of the federal government. Five years later I received my final award letter indicating that a settlement of compensation had been reached – it was anticlimactic. It was a bittersweet victory after having fought so long for what I deserved. I found myself left wondering how many other veterans were not as fortunate when confronted with such an onerous task; no wonder so many fail to secure their legitimate benefits and wind up living under bridges.

Key West, Florida
Early 2000's

Early one morning while vacationing with friends in Key West, Florida, I sought out a quiet spot on a beautiful beach, alone, as I would often do to reconnect with myself. I sat beside some large boulders that created a jetty and listened to the quiet affections of the waves as the early morning sun sought me out. I closed my eyes in contemplation of my surroundings. The sand beneath my feet reminded me of my connection to the earth. My toes sank deep into the cool particles; I felt safe, comfortable, and at home. The tide brought the ocean closer, moving it forward ever so slowly as if it were a cautious lover caressing the shore. Wave after wave climbed inland; those overanxious collided with one another along the beach, their last words creating a soft goodbye as they fell away and receded in one grand sweeping motion. How simple, how enjoyable, are such things of unending inconsequence; they are like the perpetual consoling intentions of the Creator toward man. He speaks His words in infinite ways, a personal message to all – specific, clear, and uplifting. If only we could hear. There, for a moment, I became one with the ocean. I left the shores of myself, unburdened of the restraints of ego and materialism, to be bathed in the light of pure consciousness.

Mysterious are the pillars of Creation which support the world in which I dwell. An architect of great wisdom and power has created the stage upon which I perform. Here on this beach, in this moment, I take my cue from my director. *How can I perform to bring credit to the role He has written for me?* My script, already written for a role of a lifetime, is familiar, albeit unclear. I have stumbled through my lines, at times trying to adlib in search of a new direction, a change of course. I have a taste for knowledge and want to consume all scripts, but I am only capable of performing one role at a time. So small am I; yet so vast is the stage. I see, but I see so little as the lights blind my eyes to an audience of unknowns. I hear, but so many sounds escape me. I know there is so much more to be known; and I feel so much more is yet to be felt. I have reached out to the props and my fellow performers in a quest to grasp some meaning. I wonder if perhaps I have missed a cue, a call, or a line. I smell a certain changing fragrance of Creation and wonder if what I sense is real. Placed upon this stage with no formal training, with no memory of acting, my direction comes from a voice off to the side; I rely on the occasional supportive nod, casual prompting for forgotten lines, and simple gestures in reminder of stage direction to keep me on track as I move forward with my script. Not all assembled on this stage are of the same mind – dutiful, kind, and willing to work together. Not all of the scenes in which I must participate are ones I would choose to repeat; but, alas, my script has been written, and it is my role to embrace.

A lone fisherman, upon entering the serenity of the scene, aroused me from my reverie with a simple, "Good morning." Opening my eyes, I responded in kind with a nod of my head. I found a satisfying feeling within the momentary recognition between our two souls. I didn't know the fisherman, but I knew many things about him as we share in this world. He was a man, flesh and blood, with an awareness of this Creation. We draw in the same air to satisfy our lungs. He fills his senses – his stomach, mind, and soul – with life, consuming those things this world has to offer. Desires are his companions; they rise and fall with the pulse of his heart and dictate his direction. His life, pure in essence, is now what he has made it. Casting his intentions far from shore, he seeks to capture something unseen. And he waits...patiently, he waits. The ocean is vast, and what he seeks may not be what he finds. I fish with countless thoughts secured to my minds' reel, with the threads of hope cast far beyond the things I know. And I, too, wait...patiently, I wait.

East Stroudsburg, Pennsylvania
Late 1990's

My father's thinking always seemed to parallel a notion held by many of the Native American tribes that once ruled this land: the more powerful your adversary, the higher your status. The prestige of a tribe was dependent on the strength of its enemies; and so it was for my father. Never willing to back down from a fight, even when the anticipated outcome was clearly not in his favor, my father seemed to relish each new contest that would come his way with an increasing level of vigor commensurate with his opponents' eminence. The greatest battles many of us will ever fight are those that take place within ourselves, where we – as our own worst enemies – can clearly see our own vulnerabilities and, therefore, launch preemptive strikes in defeat of plans before they ever have a chance to manifest.

I recall having once become embroiled in a dispute with a major insurance company when they reneged on an agreement we had reached after my employment had been terminated. I had always managed myself in an easy-going manner, so much so that I was often mistaken for being a pushover. I would tolerate a lot, but I could become a difficult adversary when my limit was reached. So it was with this rock of a company that wielded its power from a hidden place while its minions, clothed in suits of legitimacy, dictated how things would be. I contested their position, armed only with our disregarded agreement and my will to receive fair treatment. Feeling marginalized by their intimidation sparked something deep inside me; it was something I had inherited from my father – the need to be treated in a civil manner.

I happened onto an advocacy group in Washington, D.C., that would assist ordinary citizens in challenging major corporations. After explaining my situation, they agreed to help me in the battle against my Goliath. They connected me with a heavyweight law firm in the Midwest; one I could never have afforded. The firm reviewed my case and agreed to take it *pro bono*. What followed was a protracted lesson in litigation with, as my brother Fred would have said, "The Man." All of our business was conducted via phone and Fed-Ex, including our depositions. Failing to reach an agreement, a court date was scheduled. With only days to spare before our appearance in court, I received word from my attorney that the insurance company wanted to settle. What annoyed me most was their obvious intention to try to wear me down over the course of so many months. I could see that the use of time was a weapon in the arsenal of the powerful, and I resented the tactic. We went back and forth until, at the very last moment, we finally reached a sizeable settlement. Given the fact that they had already run me around for a year, I did have a caveat: I wanted the payment to be in cash. They told me that they would either give me a cashier's check or do a direct deposit, but I insisted on cash or the deal was off. After some wrangling, they conceded; but they told me (perhaps in an attempt at discouragement) that I would have to go to a bank in Washington, D.C., to retrieve the money myself. Although D.C. was a five-hour drive from my home in Pennsylvania, I immediately agreed.

My wife and I took the long drive. When we arrived, I went into the bank while she waited in the parked car outside. Believing all would go smoothly, I sought out the person I was to meet. The teller told me, "I am sorry, sir, but he is not available and cannot be reached. I have a note that you were coming, and I will write out a cashier's check." *Oh, really.* As shades of Mean Mike began to envelop my scorched sensitivities, I explained that had not been the agreement. I raised my voice to a level far beyond that of normal conversation; the acoustics in the stately old bank amplified my volume all the more. Managing to draw the attention of the bank guards and everyone else within hearing range, I made no attempt to hide the reason for my demands. My long battle to this point had been faceless; but now, with a body in front of me, I felt compelled to voice my frustration. I delivered a short rant filled with disparaging remarks. The bank guards encouraged me to lower my voice and settle down as they escorted me to a meeting room. Emboldened by a sense of righteousness, I demanded to speak to someone of authority to resolve the situation. That didn't happen; instead, I was told they would submit to my request. I spent an awkward twenty minutes with the bank guard who was left to keep me company. I imagined my wife, sitting outside with the engine running, must have been growing concerned that I had managed to get into some trouble. When the cash was finally brought in, it was placed in front of me on the large meeting room table. I was asked to count it in front of those present. I began counting the cash; but, mindful of the bazaar spectacle I had already created, I quickly grew uncomfortable under the intent observation of those witnessing my slow tallying. Confident that this much money could not have made it this far unless it had been counted several times, I stopped my count after some few thousand and agreed to sign off on the correct amount being received. I asked if they could supply me with a bag, which they did; I piled the cash into the bag and thanked them for their help as I left the room. When I got back outside to the car, I jumped into the passenger seat, gave my patiently waiting wife a kiss, and locked the doors. I felt that the whole drama was a small victory played out with a modicum of insanity. I knew my father would have enjoyed the competition.

When telling my mother about the trip to D.C., she shocked me by saying, "You are just like your father – unpredictable and idealistic." My mother was an angel on this earth, and her words were always heartfelt, honest, kind, and forgiving. In a way I was glad that her comparisons, although justified, went no further than they did. It always scared me to hear of (or to see in myself) my similarities to my father. We were very different people; yet it is unavoidable not to share the spirit, if not the machinations, of your parents.

Staten Island, New York
2014 (looking back to the 1960's)

At 89 years old, my mother was still sharp. While enjoying a cup of tea with her one afternoon, she wondered if she had ever told me about the financial boon that had found its way into our home decades earlier. She said, "It's a story your father and I always kept to ourselves."

As it turned out, a few years after we moved to 955 Richmond Road, our family had been struggling to make ends meet. No stranger to hard times, when my mother said things were tough, I knew they must have been downright bad. I didn't remember feeling a sense of desperation at that or any other time; things simply were as they were. I attribute the feeling of stability to my mother's way of adapting to adversity, providing us the luxury of her enduring peace. She had taught us to make the most of whatever we had and to hold on to the optimism of change that insured things would not remain as they were. Apparently, however, things were so slow in the construction industry that winter that we were unsure of how we were going to pay our bills; our situation had become desperate.

As my father was out of work and needing to stay busy, my mother would find odd jobs around the house to keep him occupied. One morning she had asked him to move a horsehair mattress that she had picked up at an auction house into one of the upstairs bedrooms. Once in place on the bed, she noticed a peculiar lump in the mattress that she tried to persuade away by repeatedly banging on it. The bump relented until, suddenly, something popped out of the side of the mattress and hit the floor. Looking down, she was shocked to see a huge roll of cash held together with a string; it was the size of a grapefruit. Panicked, she picked it up. It was hard to tell how much money she was holding, but she knew it was a lot. She called down the hall to my father, in a voice reserved and urgent at the same time. She waved for him to come quickly. Unnerved by her peculiar behavior, he asked, "What the hell is going on?" When she showed him the roll of cash and told him it had fallen out of the mattress, his response was "Holy shit!" As though someone else might hear, she quietly asked him what they were going to do. My father then proceeded to pull off the string and toss the cash into the air in a celebratory gesture resulting in a shower of every denomination covering the room; he joyfully repeated the process over and over. When the initial shock of finding the money passed, she said they began in earnest to collect and count the find. Time and again they counted, making neat piles of $100 across the floor. The final tally was $4,640. That was a lot of money back then. My mother said they felt that it was some sort of divine intervention to ease our financial woes; and they were thankful – ever so thankful. Getting caught up on the rent and paying back some friendly loans allowed them to breathe a little easier. They had never told anyone about their discovery because of some undetermined fear that the find was not their own. She ended the story simply by saying, "All these years later, the thought of our good luck brings a smile to my face."

East Stroudsburg, Pennsylvania
Early 2000's

In the movie *Forrest Gump,* when Tom Hanks (as the title character) is asked why he was inexplicably running across the country, he responds, "I just felt like running." Similarly, one day *I just felt like writing*…and so I began writing a book that would be ten years in the making. A magazine article I once wrote about my time in Cambodia served as my primer into the world of wordsmiths. I had no previous interest in or talent for writing; what I did manage to put on paper was always in need of heavy editing, but I did have a lot to say. I began my book in earnest, never fully expecting to finish it, let alone get it published.

A writer I encountered along the way gave me some guidance on how to channel my thoughts. He said, "You have to look at the book like you're building a house. The book's foundation is your commitment to telling a story. The house itself is an expression of your vision of the war in Vietnam and Cambodia as only you saw it. The rooms within the house are the chapters – some big, some small, each with a different expression. So pick a blueprint for a house that seems appropriate for who you are. Make it a place where you would want to live. Build its rooms (its chapters) and decorate them with your thoughts." So, with my blueprint in mind, I began construction at the very kitchen table where many a Moynihan venture had seen its beginning.

Fighting Shadows in Vietnam was a project – a mild obsession – always waiting patiently for me to build further. At times my building materials were scarce and production was slow, but there were other times when sudden bursts of creative enthusiasm would bring the edifice closer to completion. Many rooms were built only to be torn down and built again. Bad weather, mental permits, and fear of what I was building would occasionally plague me; of course there was also the fear of rejection. After eight years of construction, however, I finally placed the roof on my house. With the help and support of family and friends, I had reached the end of the story.

The pile of faded yellow legal pads, with what my wife referred to as her "husband's hieroglyphics," were all transcribed into a digital format. Though many of my hastily-scribbled ideas were illegible or coffee-stained from my writing sessions at Dunkin Donuts and so never quite found their way into the final story, I had completed a structure that housed my thoughts, my experiences, and my vision of war. I could now invite the general public to view my mental real estate. Memories, the touchstones of my story, lined the walkway to my front door. Once inside, readers could pass through the rooms I had constructed and reflect upon the furnishings from my past. They could open the closet doors and peer into dark spaces, or sit before a fireplace radiating stories of those who had sacrificed their lives. They could sit on the front porch listening to an old man as he brushed the dust from memories shelved half a century ago. They could experience the chaotic world in which I lived.

Writing the story had occasionally proved difficult and depressing – even poisonous – but it had also been fun and cathartic. Unbeknownst to me at the time, publishers usually will not deal with unknown authors directly. I needed to have an agent. In my search for representation, I learned that agents are very selective about whom they represent; most would not even respond to manuscript submissions. It was suggested that I self-publish, but I didn't feel quite right about going in that direction. I suppose, fueled by ego, I sought some recognition. I continued searching for publishers who would accept unsolicited submissions and finally managed to get McFarland to agree to review my work. About a month after anxiously submitting my manuscript, while feeling the process was moving along smoothly, I received a demolition letter that tore apart the house I had built. They were to the point and kind in their criticism, but it was extensive: the story needed to be fuller; it needed to be longer; it needed further editing; they didn't like the ending; it needed a catchier title; along with a cache of other recommendations meant to improve upon what I thought I had perfected. The letter concluded with this affirmation: "Nice try for your first attempt at writing." Initially, I was so disappointed that I was tempted to scrap the project completely; however, after some thought, I ultimately yielded to my previous determination to see it through to the end. I summoned my enthusiasm and put together a plan to renovate, to rewrite the book. It was a task that turned out to be larger than I had first envisioned. Writing a book had been a lot of work, but I found rewriting a book to be torture. Every word I altered created a ripple of change throughout the entire manuscript.

An unintended consequence of writing the book came when I wanted to insert pictures of those with whom I had served. The publisher told me that I would need a written release from anyone whose picture appeared in the book for liability reasons. With that in mind, I set about trying to contact people with whom I had no connection for 35 years. Many of the names I could recall, but there were some who had always been referenced by their nicknames (their given names lost in the process); with the help of the internet, I was able to track most of them down. It was unintentional, but I soon found that my phone calls to old friends put me in a position of rekindling traumas from their pasts. Most conversations would begin with a long pause or an expletive of surprise. Some calls would go on for over an hour, with periods where our now-older voices would falter in the emotions that we, as young men, had always managed to conceal. Some calls were abrupt, ending with a quick goodbye after telling me they didn't want to talk about Vietnam as they had put the whole experience far behind them. Whether or not they agreed to allow their pictures to be used, I respected their wishes.

My contacts would often lead to new names and more (sometimes disturbing) information. In one case I had contacted someone who, as it turned out, lived but a few hours away; we decided to get together. Our meeting was agreeable at first, but before long, as we began to discuss the deaths of different soldiers, it took on a dark air. In an awkwardly forceful way, he blurted out that he was responsible for the explosion in Cambodia that had resulted in the critical wounding of two sergeants and the death of our lieutenant. The men of whom he spoke were Batman, Frenchy, and Lieutenant Morgan, the latter being the officer whose spirit had consoled me about this very incident during my reading with Clara many years before. Shocked by his revelation, I shamelessly sought more information from the wound now reopened in his memory. As he bled out details, I was unable to stem the long-festering flow of pain; I just listened in disbelief as he relived the situation. The explosion, their screams for help, and the discovery of their bodies – these very same images that he had held close for so long – were all just as clear in my mind's eye as I had been present for the deadly incident myself. The clarity of his recall bore witness to the number of times he had relived the tragic event. Visibly upset, his remorse was contagious. I assured him that his role in the accident was part of the circumstance of war – accidents occurred all too frequently, often with tragic results. I thanked him for sharing this long-secreted story with me. Whether it was helpful for him to share what he had carried for so long in silence, I could not tell; but it left me to rewrite my own memories with new information that our lieutenant had died because of the actions of one of his own men. We ended our meeting with assurances of getting together again, both of us knowing a future meeting was unlikely. I think we both wanted to distance ourselves from the scene of the conversation, to try to push the thoughts expressed back into the past.

As we sat there speaking, sharing in words these painful images from Vietnam, we were seemingly surrounded with the essence of those about whom we spoke. I felt as though we had been resurrecting the dead. By my actions, I had initiated unsettling events; I wondered if what I was doing was of any help to those I had contacted or, for that matter, to myself. It was a strange experience to talk with these men so many years later. Each of them had moved on, but their youth, like my own, remained anchored in Vietnam.

My last – and most troubling – search was for the lieutenant who had taken the place of Lieutenant Morgan after he was killed in the accident in Cambodia. Lieutenant John Cramer was a leader to whom I had felt a strong connection. I was unable to locate a phone number for him and so began mailing letters to possible addresses around the country. One evening I heard from another officer who had been in my unit; he told me that he had recently spoken to the distressed wife of Lieutenant Cramer. She had received my letter and was upset because her husband had vanished mysteriously some years earlier; she thought my letter was somehow connected to his disappearance. As the story unfolded, I was shocked to learn that, not long after his discharge, he had returned to Vietnam as a mercenary. I could find no logical reason why he would go back, except for the irrational behavior that I had witnessed and read about regarding soldiers upon their return from combat; after Vietnam some simply could not adjust to the life they once knew and, thus, returned to war seeking the familiar comfort and deep camaraderie they had known in combat. It was a place where they seemed to belong, where they felt whole. The rush of adrenaline from living close to death was more powerful than any narcotic. It was twisted, perverted thinking to those not familiar with such bonds, but it was a draw understood by those who had served. I learned that Lieutenant Cramer had survived Southeast Asia for a second time. Upon his return home, he had found his way to a cigar boat off the southeast coast of Florida. With the booming demand for drugs in the U.S. and his need for adventure, he had begun making clandestine runs through the dangerous blue waters off the Bahamas and the Cuban mainland. That lifestyle, too, had eventually taken its toll; looking for his final score, he set off on what was to be his last trip, never to return. His fate unknown, he was likely a casualty of the perilous endeavors surrounding that life. *Such a waste*, I thought on hearing of his misfortune.

The result of this last search brought an end to my desire to reestablish connections with the faces from my past – I found the venture too painful. Unable to get the signatures required for publication from all those in my pictures, I decided to proceed without them. After another two years of rewriting, I resubmitted my completed manuscript to McFarland. Ultimately, it was accepted and published a year later. It had been cathartic to unload my mental baggage, and the feeling of accomplishment to have actually written a book was beyond satisfying.

***

Shortly before the book was published, I had an experience that scared me into realizing that I might have never seen it released. Of all the terrifying things, real or imagined, that I have experienced in this life, none has been more disconcerting than the onset of amnesia. The painfully unaware forfeiting of my self-awareness, while the world around me continued, occurred on an otherwise peaceful Saturday morning. While my wife was away on a trip with her sister, I was spending the day working on a project in the basement with my oldest son, Chad. We were drilling a hole in the basement floor to install a vent when I, as my son explained it, "began to act peculiar." Apparently, I had started continually asking him what we were doing and was soon walking around in a state of confusion, repeating myself all the while. Concerned that I might be having a stroke, or that maybe I was losing my mind, he tried to get me to a nearby hospital; I refused to get in the car. After threatening that he was going to call for an ambulance, he said I finally relented and took the short ride to the emergency room. Unable to answer a basic series of questions once there, I was rushed before a number of doctors and given a battery of tests to determine if I was, in fact, having a stroke. After a few hours of evaluation, the doctors told my son that I was experiencing something called Transient Global Amnesia (TGA): an uncommon state resulting in a failure to retain the passing moments that make up our lives. They were unsure of what its origins might have been in my case as it could be brought on by any number of catalysts. The doctors told my son that I would have no recollection of events past the onset of the TGA, but that I would gradually regain my awareness (as is usually the case) within 24 hours. They said I should feel normal within a few days, without any continuing deficits. A follow-up visit with a neurologist was also recommended. With that, I was discharged and brought home. Eight hours later, feeling as though I was waking up despite being in a conscious state, I found myself sitting in my usual seat at the head of the table. As they were watching me intently, I could only ask my concerned family, "What happened?" They asked if I was all right, and I said, "I think so. What the hell happened? Did I fall and hit my head?" They informed me that we had gone to the hospital where I had been diagnosed with Transient Global Amnesia. "What the hell is that? I've never heard of it? I feel like I was knocked unconscious."

I noticed that my other two sons, Jonathan and Michael, were at the table; I asked why they were here and when they had arrived. Apparently, Chad had called them, saying that they should get up to the house given my wacky behavior. Relieved to see I was returning from whatever place I had been for most of the day, they played out the events that had taken place. I was not yet fully myself, but I was able to understand and, just as important, able to remember. Still not feeling completely clear-headed, I sensed a feeling somewhat like a hangover. I was uncomfortable from the prolonged stares of concern as my family watched closely for any sign of a recurrence while we ate dinner. I tried to persuade myself that everything was okay. My true discomfort, which I did not voice, was my unfamiliarity with my diagnosis. *What is Transient Global Amnesia? How did it happen? Why did it happen? Could it happen again? And, if so, how do I prevent it?*

I asked if I had been out of control or aggressive with the doctors at the hospital, wondering if I had channeled my father's distaste for the profession. Chad said, in a nice way, that I had been "uncooperative." His wife, who was also at the table, said with a smile, "You were cursing a lot. I have never heard you curse in the house or around the grandkids, but you expressed a constant refrain of 'I don't understand what the fuck is going on.'" I was very tired and wanted the comfort of my bed to ease the stress of the day. After thanking everyone for their concern and apologizing for the day's events, I bid them all a good night. Still not feeling right, I sought out sleep as a safe haven, a neutral point in my consciousness where any deficiency I was feeling would be negated. I slept the sleep of concern and awoke the next morning trying to analyze myself. I found it hard to know if I was back to normal when it was my own awareness making the assessment. I tried to casually entertain a self-evaluation so as not to spark any unwanted influence; however, you can't sneak up on yourself. I did discover an annoying presence of random dominating thoughts that co-existed with whatever was occurring in my cognitive state; somehow I was entertaining more than one thought at a time. Throughout my life I had been told that you could not think of two things at once, but I now discovered that was not exactly true. I assured myself that it was a residual effect of the amnesia and would pass; I would just have to deal with it for now. What, if anything, had truly changed would probably be determined through my interaction with my environment.

Later that morning, I went to the kitchen where my family had already gathered around the table for breakfast. Upon entering the room, in a stupid gesture of humor meant to reduce my family's concern, I asked in a surprised voice, "Who are you people?" My poor attempt at levity was met with a collective groan of discontent; they were not amused. "Sorry," I conceded. Relieved that I seemed recovered, and for my benefit, they repeated the events of the prior day over and over. Always fearful of seeing my father's behavior in myself, especially in those moments when my guard is down, I was glad to hear that I had not been behaving like a wild man during those moments that had not found their place in my memory.

It was peculiar how significant each lost moment had become. How valuable, how irreplaceable, are these infinite still frames of our existence that accumulate to form a record of all that we are exposed to in this life; the loss of even one disrupts the chain of awareness. Like a word missing letters, a day without a morning, or a song without an end, the loss of cognition (however brief) was unsettling. I had experienced a state of consciousness without shields of inhibition – had been a being with no personality, a sleepwalker disconnected, unplugged but still operating. The antithesis of omniscient, I wondered what things there were that I no longer remembered and how I would even know that I had forgotten them. I found myself ruminating over a new-found threat, another intangible intrusion of my mind. I thought of my father in his final days in the hospital as he lay alive inside a body that was no longer his own. I wondered which was worse: to have the body working and not the mind, or vice versa.

Why is it that what we experience must be so? Such a fine line we walk while engaged in life suitably unaware of the things that might befall us, cautiously avoiding surrender to untroubled ignorance or the preoccupied pitfalls of trepidation. As I regained my sense of normalcy, I reflected upon the precious albeit perilous nature of life and the dream-like state in which we live.

It took several weeks for me to begin feeling what I thought was customary behavior, together with my new anticipatory anxiety. I was not expecting but, nevertheless, was on guard for a recurrence. I remember once during the course of my recovery stopping to consider what might have been if the amnesia had been permanent. While offering a glimpse of how susceptible we are – not just to death, but to a living death – that consideration set the stage for one of those moments in which I wished that I had done, said, or contributed something more to life. It reminded me of an epic poem by Dante Alighieri and how amnesia, invalidating an ongoing life, would be fitting the torment of those suffering in the inferno of his "Divine Comedy."

East Stroudsburg, Pennsylvania
Late 1990's

Just before the turn of the last century, my life took a distinct turn for the better. Whatever karmic payments I had made were now clearly rewarded by a peaceful and uncomplicated existence in the mountains of Pennsylvania. I had reached a point where the gift of each day brought joy, a constant reminder of the value of any given moment. Our three sons, now growing ever older, with their own families and racing forward in their lives, were a blessing. I felt blessed not to see the destructive nature of addiction manifested in my own children – not one of my boys displayed the predisposed, genetic-borne inheritance of the curse.

The years have passed slowly as I have engaged each day, and now their passing seems but an instant from the eyes of a senior. I feel that life has brandished a mystery before me with the Creator veiled before my eyes in unending, anonymous roles. As a student in His classroom of life, striving for a degree of understanding, I am satisfied with – though I have not yet given up on – my spiritual search. I will casually await and assimilate any further understanding that is to come my way.

East Stroudsburg, Pennsylvania
Thanksgiving 2014

"Come on, Mickey, get ready. The kids have just arrived, and you have to check the turkey!" Adele's voice brought me back to the moment at hand.

My flash of nostalgia complete, I returned to the present feeling content and satisfied with life. I have come to realize that I am but a mortal apprentice on a remarkable journey, a drop within the ocean of life only to one day realize that I am the ocean. Always rising and falling on the waves of evolution, swept up in the currents of consciousness as I move toward ever greater and sunnier shores, I am thankful just to be. I have found that I am at my best when I am grateful for everything – and nothing in particular – while aware and experiencing this life in all its joy and sorrow. I presume the Creator of my being would desire no more.

I could hear the voices of my grandchildren as they entered my home, sounding like golden remnants of my own children calling out from long ago. Their liveliness fills the spaces in my heart with an intangible joy, lifting my spirit and enlivening my connection with my lineage, past and present, in the process. Their priceless embraces and gemstone eyes convey the news of another generation, the construct of which is ages old, built upon the Moynihan name, tradition, and spirit.

My life – the product of my thoughts, desires, and actions – is one of my own making within the sphere of unavoidable possibilities. Shaped by fate, it could be no more or less than what it is, unworthy of recognition outside of my mandated mediocrity. Indentured by conception as a mortal apprentice, cultured through (and by) karma and free will, I have moved about this planet in search of my elusive *self*. I have surely forgotten more than I have learned as my hands have grasped at the ocean of knowledge that can so easily spill from even the most secure vessel.

***

The table was set as it had been countless times before, amidst an assembly of those souls whom I had just rekindled in my awareness. Pleased by the memories of those who had found comfort by its side, I imagined my father seated at the forefront. Thanksgiving had always been the high point of the year around this revered table. Together with my wife, family, and our unseen guests we would once again experience laughter, warmth, and energy as we gathered in fellowship to enjoy a meal and celebrate life. A safe port in the harbor of my home, the table was seated beyond capacity in silent witness to our voices, holding our stories in confidence and seemingly content to remain in service with us for generations to come...perhaps it is awaiting tales to be told of my journey in this life as seen through eyes other than my own.

I am but a mortal apprentice

auditioning upon the world's crowded stage,

evolving in a universal consciousness

while engaged in the complexities of life.

- Mickey Moynihan

Made in the USA
Middletown, DE
06 August 2016